S0-ARE-555

Grayson County Public Library
Independence, VA

IF IT WEREN'T FOR YOU, FOR YOU, WE COULD GET ALONG!

How to Stop Blaming and Start Living

Other Books of Interest

DC Press

*366 More Surefire Ways to Let Your Employees
Know They Count*

52 Ways to Live Success... From the Inside Out!

Cut the CRAP...and Resolve Your Problems

*E-R: [Employee Retention] — Taking the Lead in
Keeping the Best*

*If It Weren't for You, We Could Get Along:
Stop Blaming and Start Living*

*In Search of Ethics:
Conversations with Men and Women of Character*

*Raising Children One Day at a Time:
A Daily Survival Guide for Committed Parents*

*The Mulling Factor: Get Your Life Back by
Taking Control of Your Career*

*The One Hour Survival Guide for The Downsized:
What You Need to Know When You're Let Go*

Who Cares: A Loving Guide for Caregivers

InSync Press

*Go for the Green! Leadership Secrets from the Golf Course
(the Front Nine)*

*Retain or Retrain: How to Keep the Good Ones from
Leaving*

*Do I Stay or Do I Go? How to Make a Wise Decision
About Your Relationship*

Turning People On: How to Be An Encouraging Person

IF IT WEREN'T FOR YOU, WE COULD GET ALONG!

How to Stop Blaming and Start Living

Lewis E. Losoncy

PRESS

A Division of the Diogenes Consortium

SANFORD • FLORIDA

158.4 LOS   1000166051
Losoncy, Lewis
If it weren't for you, we coul
 d get along!

Copyright © 2003 by Lewis E. Losoncy

All rights reserved. No part of this publication may be reproduced, stored in a retrieval system, or transmitted in any form or by any means—electronic, mechanical, photocopy, recording, or any other—except for brief quotations in printed reviews, without the prior permission of the publisher.

Published by DC Press
2445 River Tree Circle
Sanford, FL 32771
http://www.focusonethics.com
407-688-1156

This book was set in Trump Medieaval
Cover Design and Composition by Jonathan Pennell

Library of Congress Catalog Number: 2001000000
        Losoncy, Lewis E.
If It Weren't For You, We Could Get Along
        ISBN: 1-932021-04-3

First DC Press Edition
10   9   8   7   6   5   4   3   2   1
Printed in the United States of America

DEDICATIONS

To Diane, Gabrielle & Tyler,

If it weren't for you …
I wouldn't fully understand love

To Albert Ellis,

If it weren't for you …
I'd still be thinking I'm an effect, not a cause

To Arnie & Sydell Miller,

If it weren't for you …

I wouldn't know that a few people can
change a whole industry

To Dennis McClellan,

If it weren't for you …

I would not have put my heart into
this book

To the Matrix Chain Gang,

All for one purpose

To the Rocky Colavito,

You taught American baseball fans that
despite all of the traders you met of the field,
you can still go on and hit hundreds of
homeruns

ACKNOWLEDGMENTS

DENNIS McCLELLAN, Publisher of DC Press, is simply a genius. Every author in the world needs to meet you. You are an author's dream.

Cindy and Marnee McClellan, for your support and friendship.

Carolyn Lea who poured her pen and her purpose into this product.

Lauren Losoncy, tennis pro, said ahead of her time. To Sue Losoncy, the wind beneath the wings.

Ron Losoncy, as Frenchman Emile Coue says, "Is getting better and better, everyday, in everyway."

My friends Len Marrella, Don Sanders, Ed Rose, Tom Chlebos, and Dick Cahn.

My teammates at Matrix Essentials, Bob Niles, David Craggs, Michael Pecce, Mary Wilson, Judie Maginn, Rob Reynolds. And to Michelle McNamee, the best there is at helping others to be their best. And to Philip Clough, my friend and Matrix's inspiration.

Ron Beible and long-time friend Paula Henry. And special thanks to Ginny Guinn.

Emily Dando, Lindsay Bell, Caroline Reese, Alex Bellows, Marjorie Berman, Colleen McNichol, Katie Ertel, Hannah Smith, Nicole Fiddler, Callie Eardley, Emily Vogel, Erika Dicky, Jennifer Kline, Jack Dando, Amelia DiPillo, Marissa DiPillo, Melanie Morris, Ashley Morris, Katie Smith, P.J. Smith, Stacey and Mallory Seigfried, Madison Smith, Kirsten Pollins, and Hallie Peterson.

Jason Strong, Craig Wolfel, Laura Gawthrop, Lauren Bollinger, Stephen Karst, Wendy Renier, and our special friend, Andrea Hamilton.

Leslie and Tom Bell, who live as close as one party away.

Thanks to all of you for your inspiration. If it weren't for you ...!

ABOUT THE AUTHOR

L EW LOSONCY IS ONE OF THE world's leading experts on encouragement. Known as "The Doctor of Encouragement," he is a psychologist and author of 17 books on the topics of encouragement, motivation, teamwork and positive attitude. Dr. Losoncy is corporate psychologist for Matrix Essentials, a division of L'Oreal, North America's largest producer of professional beauty products.

Other recent books by Losoncy include *Turning People On*; *Today: Grab it!*; *What Is, Is!* with Diane Losoncy; *The Motivating Team Leader* with Don Dinkmeyer; *The Skills of Encouragement* and *The Best Team Skills*.

"Dr. Lew" has spoken in all 50 United States, most of the Provinces of Canada, throughout Australia and New Zealand, as well as Mexico, France, and England. He has appeared on *CNN* and *CBS This Morning* and in media as varied as *The Wall Street Journal*, *Psychology Today*, and *Talk*.

He lives in Wyomissing Pennsylvania, with his wife Diane and his daughter Gabrielle.

PUBLISHER'S COMMENT

WITH 60,000 BOOKS being pumped out annually in this country, it is difficult to find those that can stand out from the crowd— those that can make you really think or provide you with real food for thought and supply tools for making significant changes in your life. Lew Losoncy has created such a book.

The central theme behind the books that DC Press publishes is simple: we want to provide the reading public with ways of impacting their own lives (as well as those they come in contact with), making changes, and influencing others — all within ethically acceptable ways. It is our sincere hope that our publications will offer encouragement to readers, while supplying an element of spirit and building character, making it clear that nothing is done without volition.

Dr. Losoncy has been speaking to and writing for hundreds of thousands of people across the United States and in many countries around the world for the past two decades. His focus has always been that one can improve his or her own lot in life by accepting that "what is, is" and that by taking responsibility for the things that one does and for the things that one can change, life can be generally better and more rewarding. It is his strong belief that even under the worst of conditions and even when facing terrible situations, an individual can still be true to themselves and show strength of character and positive decision-making skills.

One need not be buried under the rubble that others create. Dr. Losoncy shows throughout this book that blame can be a terminal illness. Some just never survive. Others, on the other hand, seem to have the skills (similar to strong antibodies that fight disease) to overcome and surmount obstacles that can cause personal defeat and life-long feelings of failure and inadequacy. Throughout the pages of *If It Weren't For You, We Could Get Along* readers will find one practical suggestion after another for taking control of what goes on around them and how to add significant longevity to their lives. The techniques aren't difficult; the results can only be positive. The toughest obstacle to face is YOU. Don't let anger, frustration, and blame consume you. Take control and learn the skills of letting go. Stop the blame game and move forward immediately.

Dennis McClellan
Publisher, DC Press

PREFACE

5 Years from Now, Which Decision Will You Wish ... You Had Made Today?

Continue to ...

1. <u>Blame</u> the other person, or <u>build</u> yourself?

2. <u>Blame</u> your past, or <u>build</u> your future?

3. <u>Blame</u> your weaknesses and fears, or <u>build</u> on your strengths and potential?

4. <u>Blame</u> the outer world, or <u>build</u> your inner confidence?

5. <u>Blame</u> reality, or <u>build</u> your frustration tolerance?

6. <u>Blame</u> people at home or work, or <u>build</u> yourself as an encourager?

7. <u>Blame</u> that huge challenge in front of you, or <u>build</u> yourself to conquer it?

Whatever your choice, 5 years from now will arrive, very soon ...

> *Blaming will find you right where you are today ...*
>
> *Building yourself will give you 5 more years of life. And then some.*

This book will develop your practical intelligence to stop blaming and start building yourself.

CONTENTS

INTRODUCTION
We Give Our Power Away to Whatever We Blame!

You have you!

And you have now!

How will you use this power full moment?

1. To find things, in your outer world, to blame...or

2. To find ways , in your inner world, to build?

Your tomorrow is determined by your decision today, isn't it?

Since September 11, 2001, reactions to the first edition of this book have been harmonious. One letter best reflected the essence of many of the other responses I received. A California woman wrote:

> *These ideas in this book cleared my mind of its loud noises. I can think again. I can feel alive again! I can do something, even if I can't do everything. I got it — Dr. Lew's mes-*

sage — early in the book, and it hit me like a warm, refreshing spring breeze after a frozen winter. My past, my boss, my job, my ex, the nasty weather, the traffic hams, the stock market, and even the terrorists are no longer going to live rent free in my mind. I have to get back to living, because that's what life is for. The only thing I wonder about is how could ideas so sensible and so powerful be so simple and clear! And how could <u>one single change in me</u> produce such a positive effect on my life!

The underlined words in her letter proved that she "got it." What is there to "get?"

NOTES FROM MY OFFICE:
Finding *the Single Factor* Leading to Personal Growth & Happiness

Psychotherapists observe a common pattern present in the first session with almost every client.

Through therapy, one major change takes place.

When therapy is successful, therapists note how the last session differs from the first session.

If can be whittled down to one new approach that the client has taken to life. In the first session, the helpless, frustrated, anxious, hurt or angry client unfolds a litany of people and things in the world that they are spending their time accumulating to blame for their frenzied emotional state.

The major change? By the last session, usually none of these outside people or things in the world have changed, but the client has changed. The client has transformed him or herslf, by deciding to build their inner world, rather than blame their outside world.

I decided that it was important to cut through the many hours of agreeing with the appropriateness of the blame, with the resultant anger, hurt, pain, etc. Oh, I empathized that if that was the way they felt, they had every right to feel that way — even unto their dying days and beyond. It was their choice. I did talk with them about people that appear in this book and who had made uplifting and constructive decisions to build. Among these people was my friend Rosalie Bailey, who despite havaing cerebral palsy and a mere fourth grade education, had made the single choice to stop blaming the outer world and start building her inner world. She went on to earn three college degrees and inspire a group of people to build America's largest professional beauty product company — Matrix Essentials. She certaily had every right to spend her short life blaming, but that didn't work too well for her.

The single decision that will change your life is to get over making the outside world so important. Start building your inside world. Move forward. It will take the same amount of time — that is, this moment — to start reconstructing your future as it would to sit around analyzing your past.   You can build yourself. It starts with your decision to stop blaming.

Why does blaming hold us back? Because we give our power away to whatever we take the time to blame.   The happiest, healthiest, self-actualizing human beings have a special kind of intelligence to grab this one single decision (to stop blaming their outer world and start building their inner selves). This is a sign of Practical Intelligence.

I'd like to invite you to join me, on a journey through these pages, to build our Practical Intelligence together.

INTELLIGENCE AND PRACTICAL INTELLIGENCE

Intelligence is the speed of one's ability to make accurate connections between cause and effect. One's practical intelligence is one's ability to take effective actions in everyday life experiences based on those connections. Happiness and success are products of one's practical intelligence.

By one conversation, you can easily spot a person with high practical intelligence. This person has found an approach to life that works for him or her. Almost immediately, you sense this person's demeanor is being guided by hope. You appreciate her openness to accept and then plow through tough setbacks, experiencing only a few momentary bumps. The only remains left of the tough times are important lessons learned, sprinkled with dashes of philosophical humor. You're moved by her upbeat attitude and unbending determination to rise above the obstacles ahead in her path. You just know that she is going to make it, even against all odds.

She is quite intelligent, in a very practical way. Her approach to life is extremely effective. She has made accurate connections between her view of life, which is the cause, and the resultant quality of her life. And then she demonstrates practical intelligence by acting on her learnings.

When you think about it, you also sense something else in this person. She is wasting little or no time in building a case to blame someone, or something else, for her life. This frees her up to focus her energies forward to design her destiny. No wonder she is an optimist. She is going places.

A person with highly developed practical intelligence is taking his or her life circumstances and molding them with a workable mental attitude to move their life forward. This person is finding ways to live life, to actualize their possibilities, rather than accumulating ways to blame life.

Compare her to the person who hasn't developed his practical intelligence. He is continuously down and out. He is still "stuck" on either other people or other events (which they describe as horrible, awful, or terrible) in his life. He even elevates these people, or events, to the level of being the "cause," the undisputed source, of what he is still helplessly going through today. Its almost as if he is saying underneath, "If only it weren't for this or that, I could be successful and happy!"

The strain on his troubled face reveals the pain of carrying this heavy baggage of blame with him. You are becoming a little less quick to agree to help him lift his weighty worries. You tried that before when you agreed that he was justified in his anger or pain. Yes, he was "done in!" And perhaps you noticed that your agreement only added further support to his immobility.

Of course, he has a right to feel pain, anger, persecution, or whatever he is feeling. The issue here is not that he is justified in his anger or hurt. The question here is, "is it wise? Does blaming something or someone else help him? Will he grow? Will he get over it and bring on a new day?" Not as long as he is blaming.

You can help. How? By assisting him to develop his practical intelligence. By encouraging him to put his blame baggage down. And then to go forward. You can help him to stop blaming and start living.

People who spend their time blaming, rather than creating a new life, direct their thoughts, feelings and energy to dwell on the useless. Practically, that isn't very productive. Instead of learning from the experience, and moving forward enriched, they consume their present life in unproductive seething and hurt. You notice that the theme of their life is, "If only it weren't for …, then I could have …!"

The theme has become such a part of their life that it just never occurs to them that it was neither the event nor the person that "caused" them to be stuck, hurt or angry. Rather, the person who has developed their practical intelligence is aware that it is the belief that, "If it weren't for ...!" that is causing their misery. They know that when we blame someone or something else for our unhappiness, we, at that moment, give our power away to that person or event. Then, we have to wait for these powerful forces that pull our string to change. That approach is neither empowering, wise, or practical.

We only have two and one half billion seconds of life to live. How many of these seconds do we want to use up consumed in helplessness or revenge toward another person in this huge world of six billion people? At some transforming moment, we gain the life-changing awareness that, "Even if no one in my life changes, and even if I had this horrible past, I can take charge of my life, right here in this powerful moment called now."

How do we develop our practical intelligence quotient and bring our power back? How do we find our center? By stopping blaming and starting living!

Listen for the "if it weren't for's ...!"

Take a few seconds and think about the people near you at home or at work. What are the things or the people that they blame for making their life miserable?

- Other people

- The past

- Fears and weaknesses

- No confidence and lack of support from others

xxiv • **IF IT WEREN'T FOR YOU, WE COULD GET ALONG!**

- Reality

- The people in the workplace

- The huge challenge ahead

These may range from other people to events in their past. Or they may even be blaming their own fears, lack of confidence, bad luck, limited education, or pessimism for holding them back.

Listen carefully for the reasons why they can't be more, do more, sell more, and live more. Listen for their, "If it weren't for's ..."

"If it weren't for _____ ,_____ ,_____ ,_____ , etc.,

I could be _____ !"

Does Blaming = Giving Power Away?

It is vital for you to stop for a moment and think. As you think about their belief you may experience the awesome power they have given to these people and experiences they are blaming. These blame sources have power over them only because they have given them power in the form of blame.

Who we blame, "if it weren't for ...!," we give our power to because we are saying, "I absolutely can't be happy, successful, positive, etc. until YOU change." My well-being depends on YOU! YOU control me! So I must wait, and wait, and wait. Blame, and blame, and blame.

BLAMING IS INACCURATE

In addition to giving power away, blaming is inaccurate. It seems that if something like blaming is both ineffective and inaccurate, then it isn't very wise to continue doing it.

How is blaming inaccurate? Look again at those blame sentences you listed. Did those blame sources automatically create the resultant attitude? If 1,000 people all experienced the same horrible setbacks from those rotten people and tragedies, would all 1,000 people be equally upset? Or would there be a range of reactions from total devastation on one hand to self-determination, motivation, and renewal on the other?

Is it possible that two different people experiencing the same event will respond to the event in two different ways, resulting in two different outcomes?

Who will walk away more happy and successful?

The one who blames ("if it weren't for ...!") or the one who is creative? "Because of that experience, I learned that I am going to do this or that. Without that experience I would not have learned this same information."

Blaming not only gives away power, but blaming is inaccurate because the event did not cause my attitude. I cause my attitude toward the event. Notice the accurate and effective connection between cause and effect: I cause my effect of bouncing back quickly from that difficult experience. I cause the effect I get.

For me, the two most significant people of the past century who helped us realize our practical intelligence power were psychiatrist Alfred Adler and psychologist Albert Ellis. Adler, in the early part of the century, concluded that neither heredity nor environment determine us. They are just the building blocks that we construct to design ourselves. When we blame, we act "as if" we live in a faulty building and we can't do anything about it until the builder comes back, apologizes, and rebuilds us a mansion. Then we could be happy.

Albert Ellis is founder of Rational-Emotive-Behavioral Therapy (REBT) and co-author of numerous books, including the life-changing *A New Guide to Rational Living*. Ellis, who is considered by the popular *Psychology Today Magazine* to be one of the leading thinkers of the last century, argued that life is as simple as A-B-C.

A is an Activating event. Someone does something to us that activates us to think about the event.

C is our Consequent emotion.

Before Ellis, we thought **A**, the Activating event, caused **C**, our Consequent emotion. But, as we stated before, events don't cause emotions because if many people all experience the same **A**, they will have different reactions at **C**.

What then caused **C** or our Consequent emotion?

The answer is **B** or our Belief about **A**. And we are in control of determining our belief. We are in control of our life. If at **B**, we believe we should blame **A**, we will be hurt or angry at **C**. If, however, at **B**, we begin to move on with what Ellis calls, Rational Thinking, then at **C**, or at our Consequent emotion, we create different results.

WOULD I THEN BE HAPPY IF THESE THINGS I BLAME DIDN'T HAPPEN TO ME?

Blaming also is inaccurate because it assumes that if these things had not happened to the person, then they would be happy and successful. Think about a person's sources of blame and ask yourself the question, "If these sources of blame were not there, would this person truly be what they think they could have been? Would it have been guaranteed?"

Of course not!

EITHER YOU DETERMINE YOUR ATTITUDE OR SOMEONE ELSE WILL!

You are the CEO of your world. You determine what you put into it, and what you take away from it each day. You cast the only and deciding vote on how you act and react to the events and circumstances in your world. As CEO of your world, you have three major resources or attitude tools at your disposal. You direct these three attitude power tools—(1) your thoughts, (2) your emotions, and (3) your actions—to work for you or against you.

Either you determine your attitude or someone else will!

Think about it this way:

You are "one" self. Within that one self, physically speaking, you are your body. Within your one self, socially speaking, you are your relationships with others. Spiritually speaking, you are your relationship with your God.

And psychologically speaking, you are your attitude.

Consequently, your attitude toward your own self, your life, and other people has a dramatic effect upon your life. There is only one thing more powerful than your attitude.

WHAT CAN BE MORE IMPORTANT THAN YOUR ATTITUDE?

You are more powerful than your attitude. Why? You direct and determine your attitude.

You can remember very conscious moments in which you decided what your attitude was going to be towards another person, can't you? Perhaps you were angry at someone else, perhaps someone younger than you. And then, in a moment of using your practical intelligence, you paused, re-routed your blaming direction and thought something like, "Well, she sure isn't perfect. And I'm not perfect either. I'll give her a break. She's just a kid!"

Your conscious, controlling, directing self changed your attitude—and your day—around. Practical intelligence helped you. You started living rather than blaming.

Or perhaps you were running late for work, the traffic was heavy, the lights were all red, and then a major accident occured up in front. You directed your attitude to connect all of these independent, basically neutral events into a theme of "the world's out to get me — all of these things shouldn't be happening on the same day. I can't take anymore or I'm going to scream!"

In this instance, you directed your attitude to go into a blame mode: "If only it weren't for ...!"

At that moment of blaming, you gave your power away and the worst consequences were not on the outside world, but on your inside world. The decision was not an intelligent one.

Think of your "one" self as having two components— (1) you as director and (2) your attitude. Your "employees" are your thoughts, your emotions, and your actions that *you* direct.

You, as director, are your conscious, determining self. The conscious, directing you chooses and decides which course for your attitude to take.

Your attitude cannot choose. Your attitude makes your conscious choices happen. When you tell your attitude that something is impossible, or frustrating, or shouldn't be, your subconscious, compliant attitude directs its resources, thoughts, emotions, and actions into building a stronger case to support your conscious, directing choice. Again, can you remember a time you directed your attitude to go that way?

When you tell your attitude that even though the odds are against us, if we put everything together, we can do anything, your attitude responds with renewed motivation. It is vital to be aware that you choose your attitude. Can you remember a time that you directed your attitude to go this way? It worked, didn't it? That means you were using your practical intelligence.

TELL YOURSELF: "I AM THE CEO (CENTRAL EXECUTIVE OFFICER) OF MY LIFE"

I direct my "employees," my thoughts, emotions, and actions.

If I direct my attitude tools constructively, the practical results are:

1. **My Thoughts:** What I tell myself that determines my destination and develops a road map to get me to my determined destination

2. **My Emotions:** My motivational fuel to keep me energized and inspired to keep going

3. **My Actions:** My vehicle, my body, taking action and being fueled by my emotions, following the road map to a destination determined by my thoughts.

In this case I am in a fully functioning state. I am using my practical intelligence.

If, however, I allow the outside world, or THE WORLD, to determine MY WORLD by blaming ("If it weren't for ...!"), then I give away my power tools. When I don't use my practical intelligence and start giving my power away by blaming, the dynamic looks like this:

1. **My Blaming Thoughts:** "If it weren't for him, her, my boss, my past, the traffic, the weather, the President, the economy, my weaknesses, the should's and shouldn'ts, things changing so much, teenagers, old people, the Republican's, the Democrat's, etc., I could be happy."

2. **My Self-Created Emotions:** Pain, anger, hurt, revenge, helplessness, etc. (Note that the specific emotion is directly determined by our specific choice of thoughts. For example, if I blame my boss, who I make strong and powerful, then I give myself feelings of helplessness.)

3. **My Resultant Actions:** I Allow my vehicle, that is, my body, to steer off the constructive course to a goal and be re-routed by acting on my blaming behaviors. "I can't reach my goal because of this or that reason, and so I have to spend my energies taking action: fighting, resisting, passive-aggressiveness, getting others involved in my anger against my blaming source, etc."

You might note: either way my day has 60 seconds in a minute, 60 minutes in an hour, and 24 hours. And I have about 30,000 of these days of potential in my life. I have to determine how I want to spend them. That is the job of a

CEO. A lot rests on my decision to blame ("If it weren't for ...!") or to live and create.

YOU ARE THE CEO OF <u>YOUR</u> WORLD, BUT YOU ARE NOT THE CEO OF <u>THE</u> WORLD!

The mistake that many people make is that while they as leaders of their lives are the determiners of THEIR **world**, they conclude they should also be the determiners of THE WORLD. Their frustrations result from their illogical, irrational, painful, and, frankly, crazy attitude that "I should control you, and you should act the way I want you to act, rather then the way you want to act." And most people frustrate themselves by believing that events in the universe should go MY WAY, rather than THE WAY they are going.

And when people and events don't act the way I want, I will give away my power and blame them: "If it weren't for you, ...!"

This is a book about how to take charge of YOUR WORLD first. The person with a high practical intelligence quotient knows this is the surest, most practical approach to life. And when OUR WORLD is together, we can go change THE WORLD. Rather than letting THE WORLD change OUR WORLD.

1

UNDERSTANDING

Works Better Than Judging

Do you have a relationship in which you believe that if it weren't for the other person, you could get along with each other?

Is it possible the other person feels the same way?

Remember: To the other guy, you're the other guy!

Have you ever tried on someone else's glasses and everything you looked at was blurry? If so, did you tell them that their glasses were wrong and that they should throw them away? And then you reassured them that you would give them your prescription because your prescription works better?

Of course not. You wouldn't even think of choosing the lens that works best for someone else. You know that their vision is different than yours. That's why we have more eyeglass businesses than you could ever see in a lifetime. There are a couple of them in most malls alone!

You understand the fact that your prescription works best for your vision.

And their prescription works best for their vision.

And, because of this understanding, you don't work yourself up over their viewpoint, do you?

In other words, when you understand that the other person naturally has a different viewpoint than you do, and you don't take it personally, it doesn't bother you. You respect their view, even though you know it wouldn't work for you.

When you think of things this way, that is, when you understand, you find that it works better for you. When you understand, you are developing your practical intelligence. Because, again, it works better for you to understand the other viewpoint than it does to judge the other viewpoint.

Did you ever judge somebody when they saw things differently on an issue in life's landscape than you did? Did you assume that because their viewpoint was different than yours, that it proved that they were wrong?

- Was judging them effective?

- Did judging them bring you closer together?

- Did you learn new things about their view that you didn't see before?

- Did you understand them better?

- Did you grow?

We grow through our willingness to stop judging and start understanding.

CHOOSING BETWEEN JUDGING AND UNDERSTANDING

Whenever any two people talk, each person is deciding to do one of two things.

1. The first choice is to listen and to understand the other person from the other person's vantage point.

2. The second option is to judge the other person from one's own vantage point.

Person A speaks	Person B's choices
	1) Listen to understand.
	• What is her view? (perspective taking)
	• How is she looking at this?

- What is she feeling about this? (empathy)

or

2) Judge the other person from my view.

- Is she right or wrong? (from my view)

More often than not, when Person B is listening to Person A, Person B is thinking, "is she right?" or "is she wrong?" What Person B is unaware of when they are judging is that they are thinking, "according to me." They think they are judging Person A according to the universal truth. (They are also operating out of the belief, usually inaccurately, that Person A even cares.)

The judge is, in grandiose fashion, subconsciously assuming, "I have the full truth, I am the compass, the lighthouse, and I am listening to you for the sake of pointing out to you where you are wrong. Sometimes I don't even have to hear you all of the way through, and will save you words by interrupting you in mid-thought. You are lucky to have me around. Plus, you will know how far off you are from the truth just by sensing how much your ideas disagree with mine."

In other words, if we disagree, *you* have some work to do. For our relationship to succeed, *you* need to change. I don't have to change because I am right. I'm surprised and annoyed that you can't see that! As a result, we have "the blaming by judging" phenomena or "If it weren't for you, we could get along!"

DON'T UNDERSTAND TO BE NICE
TO THE "OTHER PERSON":
UNDERSTAND TO BE NICE TO "YOURSELF"

Shh! The person you disagree with didn't buy this book. You did. So while I love them as a fellow human being, I am here for you. I am not asking you to understand them because you should be nice to them, or because it will improve your relationship, or because it will take the pressure off the relationship, or because they will feel understood.

All I am saying is that the person with practical intelligence listens rather than judges because it works better for them. In other words, when you stop judging and blaming, and instead listen and understand, you begin to grow by realizing there is another vantage point, another set of eyeglasses, that can be worn to look at the same old thing. Understanding works better. And yes, understanding is only fair.

IMAGINE THE SUPREME COURT HEARING
ONLY ONE SIDE OF THE STORY

Why am I so right and you are so wrong when we disagree? Why am I so convinced of the superiority of my position? Very simply: because I live from my vantage point twenty-four hours a day.

For example, I think I have the toughest job because I know intimately all of the stresses my job has. The lazy people in the other department that are holding things up don't have the stress I have, and so I judge them and blame them. This causes resentment and anger in me. I spend most of my day thinking about my job pressure and very little time thinking about theirs. (Unfortunately the other side is as biased as I am and is doing the same thing about me.)

What if the Supreme Court of the United States of America took the same prejudiced, biased position. Imagine if one day the Chief Justice concluded, "I only need to hear one side of the story, and then I'll make my decision."

The outcry would be like an explosion. "This is America, you need to hear both sides of the story. This in unfair!"

When we judge without giving another person equal time to present their viewpoint, we are like the judge who won't allow equal time. If we spend twenty-four hours a day focusing on our side, wouldn't it be fair for us to use twelve hours and give the other side twelve?(And wouldn't the things we learn in the twelve hours they are talking be more informative and helpful to us than the things we learn from the twelve hours we are talking?)

Plus, when we judge, we are violating another great American, time-honored principle. We are operating out of the idea that the other person is guilty until proven innocent!

IS IT POSSIBLE THAT THERE IS ANOTHER VIEWPOINT OTHER THAN MY OWN?

Draw a capital letter "E." From one viewpoint, it is clearly an E.

But from other viewpoints, we can see that it could be a W or an M or even a bad comb. Now, whichever viewpoint it is depends upon one's point of view.

Can you agree with this? The person who looks to understand fully the alternate possibilities in that letter has the richest view of them all. This person can see more. This as an example of practical intelligence.

Is it possible that the person who listens to understand another's viewpoint is more enriched and grows more, while the judge only goes back to their view and continues blaming?

One very interesting experience I had was to work with a school district where conflict was deep. Almost all sides judged, blamed, and even hated the other sides because of the judging and blaming. Working with each group for three hours, I asked them to share their viewpoint of the job stresses.

The school board members told me they have to get elected, they are scrutinized by the community, their children are put down by teachers because of the low pay raise, they receive angry letters from taxpayers, etc. In three hours time, my own eyes were opened. I had no idea of the depth, importance, and stress of their work. In fact I left the meeting concluding that they actually have the toughest job in the school district. I changed my view through understanding. You might say I saw the E like a W.

Then for three hours I met with school administrators, and I opened myself up to listen to understand their viewpoint. When they told me about dealing with angry parents who only want the most popular teachers for their children, dealing with drug-related problems, breaking up fights, and working with angry teachers, as well as tough school board members, my eyes were opened again. I left this meeting thinking that this group has the toughest job in the district.

Next I met with teachers, and in three hours of understanding, I had the same experience of deep respect. This was followed by meetings with cafeteria workers, bus drivers, custodians, students, and parents. Wow, none of this was easy for anyone.

My final meeting was with parents who the teachers said butt in too much. A parent asked me, "Since we are paying for all of this, don't you think we have some rights?"

You see, having been a teacher, I intimately knew the teachers' views about all of the other groups. The blaming, the anger, the division. But now, I had a richer view. I could see things and understand things that at one time I just judged before. This was good for me. It was therapeutic for me. The value of listening to understand is not only to help the other person. The value of understanding is for me too because when I stop blaming and start understanding, my life changes.

Oh, but back to the school district. How did we resolve the conflict? By bringing everyone together, I could speak to them about what I learned. As each clique sat together, I talked to them about my insight into how much they have in common.

"I have had the opportunity to walk a mile in the shoes of everyone here in the school district and I have found that everyone in this room has so much in common."

They looked at each other with an expression suggesting that their collective sentiment was "this guy has really missed the point."

I continued, "What you have in common is that no matter what you do here in this school district, you have concluded that your group got the raw deal and all of the other groups have it made."

"This is natural because you spend twenty-four hours a day thinking about your job and very little on the jobs of your fellow community members who play a different role on your team. You then judge and blame, and this gives you further evidence of your already drawn conclusion. Then perhaps you hang out with people who do the same things that you do and have the same view as yours, and this gives you even further support. Then you go home at night and share your view with your spouse. His or her only source of input is your view, and he or she is ready to fight for you."

"There is an answer. Spend equal time on the other side of the story. You spend too much time getting a one-sided view. Reach out to listen to understand rather then to judge and blame. This will help the healing."

"And one final thing. Don't understand just to help the other person. Understand because it will help you."

THE NEGATIVE OUTCOMES OF BLAMING

When Person B judges instead of understands Person A's message, Person B may cut off a lot of potentially valuable and honest information. This is information from which Person B can learn, but Person B misses the learning opportunity. Let's consider a number of disadvantages when we judge rather than listen to understand another.

1. We miss information.

2. We frustrate the other person who is unable to communicate the desired message to us without our judgmental interference.

3. We receive a distorted message, minus details that the speaker believes we don't want to hear or we can't handle.

4. We hear inaccurate information because the other person tells us what he or she believes we want to hear.

5. We anger the other person when we judge because he or she feels we are condescending, judgmental, and paternal.

These are just a few of the many, many deleterious effects of choosing to judge and blame rather than to listen to understand another. No wonder a person who seeks to understand, a rare but valued phenomenon, becomes more effective with people. Communication with a person who sensitively understands becomes cleaner, clearer, honest, and enjoyable.

UNDERSTANDING DOESN'T MEAN AGREEING

Some people make the error of concluding that because they are listening to understand someone that it means they are agreeing with them. Nothing is further from the truth. Non-judgmental listening is one process that focuses on under-

standing the other person's *viewpoint from the other person's world.* Judging involves listening to the other person
to *understand the other person from the judge's world.* So,
we can simultaneously understand another person fully and
disagree with the other person completely.

Non-judgmental listening is neither agreeing nor disagreeing because it is an attempt to hear without the foggy
interference of one's own viewpoint. In this way the other
person's message becomes more accurate and real.

Please note that while we are uncovering the disadvantages of blaming in this book, because it hurts the blamer,
we are not taking a stance against judging. You will learn
how to effectively confront people later on in our discussion
on assertiveness. There is a time for disagreeing. At the time
for disagreeing, we want to have a clear understanding about
what we are disagreeing about. That clear understanding
comes through our non-judgmental listening. Plus, when
we disagree with a solid understanding of the other person's
viewpoint, our assertive communication becomes even
more effective.

DE-HUMANIZING IS
A FORM OF JUDGING AND BLAMING

"You people in the office have no idea about what's going on
out there in production."

"The Democrats will raise your taxes every time."

De-humanizing occurs when we relate to another as if "I'm a person, you're a thing." We reduce the other person or group to a single feature. For example, "he's the janitor" or "you people in sales are all the same." In de-humanizing, we erroneously conclude that (1) all of them think exactly alike, and (2) the way they think is different and inferior to me.

When two countries are at war, both de-humanize the other by labeling each other which has the effect of making the other less than a person—more like a thing. Can you kill an animal? Then maybe you can see the connection between judging, blaming and de-humanizing.

De-humanizing is overcome be re-humanizing. Re-humanizing occurs when we first see the other person as a person and then let the other person's viewpoint in. It's like thinking, "This person is a person just like me. And like me, this person has some viewpoints about life. It would be helpful to me to listen to understand and to learn about this fellow human's viewpoint. If this other person does the same with me, we can learn from each other."

When the sales people and the accounting people de-humanize each other—"sociopathic salespeople" and "anal bean counters"—re-humanization is the answer. The result of re-humanizing would have each concluding that "true, each of us, one in sales and one in accounting have different responsibilities, but each of us are people who (1) have many things in common with each other and (2) differ in many ways from those who have the same responsibilities as we do."

In *The Brighter Side of Human Nature*, Alfie Kohn suggests that the way we get beyond isolated group membership and move toward re-humanizing is to conclude:

> *"She may be one of them, but she is mostly*
> *(1) a person like me, and (2) an individual,*
> *distinct from the others in her group."*

In the process of re-humanizing, the other person becomes a person, like me, a person who I am beginning to understand has viewpoints, ideas and feelings. And we are a step closer to realizing the absurdity of a statement such as, "If it weren't for you, we could get along."

WHAT CAN WE DO TO BUILD MUTUAL UNDERSTANDINGS?

In *On Becoming a Person*, psychologist Carl Rogers points out how judgment is the major obstacle to mutual understanding, and then offers a solution to overcome the barrier.

> *"... the major barrier to mutual interpersonal communication is our very natural tendency to judge, evaluate, approve or disapprove, the statements of the other person or group. Although this tendency to make evaluations is common in almost all interchanges of language, it is very much heightened in those situations where feelings and*

emotions are deeply involved. So the stronger our feelings, the more likely it is that there will be no mutual element in communication. This tendency to react to any emotionally meaningful statement by forming an evaluation of it from our own point of view is, I repeat, the major barrier to interpersonal communication."

"But, is there any way of solving this problem, of avoiding this barrier? Real communication occurs, and this evaluative tendency is avoided when we listen with understanding. What does this mean? It means to see the expressed idea and attitude from the other person's point of view, to sense how it feels to him, to achieve his frame of reference in regard to the thing he is talking about."

Understanding isn't easy. It isn't for everyone. To truly understand, it has been observed by Alfie Kohn that one needs intelligence, cognitive development, imagination, mental health, flexibility, generosity of spirit, and openness.

But the rewards of understanding build bridges to the rich lands of others, giving us opportunities to see new vistas, so that when we return to our perceptual homeland, we are enriched forever.

SKILLS AND STRATEGIES TO UNDERSTAND

Communicating Your Desire to Understand the Other Person

To enrich your life through understanding another person, start with a determination inside your heart to create a safe, understanding climate for the other person. And next, and this will be more difficult, resist the natural tendency to interrupt, judge, and blame.

Show your presence in the relationship. You show your presence when you create an atmosphere in which others feel safe to discuss their concerns. You are present by providing time and by attending to their needs. You show an interest in what concerns them. You are making an unselfish commitment to hear them. Your physical presence involves eye-to-eye contact, warmth, and a relaxed, open body posture.

Eye Contact

Effective listeners have the ability to use an ideal amount of eye contact when communicating. What is ideal? Obviously, too little or no eye contact might be perceived as disinterest. On the other hand, constant staring may be threatening and produce defensiveness in the speaker. The ideal amount is one with which you feel comfortable, but which has few breaks in contact. When you are truly listening, your body confirms that.

Another function of eye contact is to convey your empathy for the other person's concerns. Often when we interrupt people while they are speaking, they lose their train of thought. By conveying through your eyes that you are in touch, you communicate your presence without distracting interruption.

Warmth and Open Body Language

A warm person has natural verbal and body language skills that communicate genuine interest—a caring and safe reception to another person. A warm person (1) centers on the other person's interests, (2) communicates moment-to-moment involvement through their facial expressions, (3) presents oneself with open body language, (4) blocks out all other distractions, and (5) is "with" the other person.

Think of warm people you know and model some of their qualities. Warmth is crucial to the understanding climate.

Listening for the Person's Theme

Effective listening involves a desire to thoroughly understand the theme of the speaker's message. This theme can be understood in a variety of ways. Focus on the speaker's view and feelings as well as the person's body language.

Listening for the Person's View (Perspective Taking)

Let in the other person's viewpoint. If asking questions, let them flow from the thought: how can I get a clearer picture of how she is looking at this issue? What is her perspective? What is her viewpoint? Is there a larger theme here? Then play back to the other person your understanding of their perspective.

"Does it look like this?"

"Let me see this clearly."

Listening for the Other Person's Feelings (Empathy)

In addition to understanding the other person's perspective, non-judgmental listening involves a sensitivity to the other person's feelings. Ask yourself, "what is this person feeling about these events and issues?" And then reflect some of those feelings back to check for accuracy.

"Were you excited?"

"Sounds like your feelings were hurt."

Observing the Other Person's Body language

People communicate in many ways. In addition to their words, ideas, and feelings, their body language can either support the accuracy of what they are saying (congruent) or there may be a discrepancy that you observe, for example, if someone says, "I am really mad at my boss" while smiling. To truly understand, you want to be fully present, safe, warm, sensitive, and in tune with the words and feelings of the other person.

In conclusion, through understanding another person, we begin to sense that he, like me, has a vantage point. And it would be most helpful for me to understand his vantage point because I will stop judging and start growing. Our task is to understand each other.

The skills and strategies here are designed to help you to resolve conflicts so that you never cause pain and anger for yourself again with the blaming words, "If it weren't for you, we could get along."

Ask if you can wear the glasses of the person you disagree with and see how things look. And, if the person doesn't wear glasses, and you do, ask the person to try glasses like yours. Looking through another person's glasses could change your life.

Understanding adds to developing our practical intelligence because we get better results. We can further develop our practical intelligence by stopping blaming and stopping making our past powerful and instead focusing on living in the present and building our future.

2

LIVING TODAY

Gets Us Over Blaming Yesterday

One of my patients looked at me, with a body language revealing helplessness, and explained, "I've had the worst past you could ever imagine."

I responded, "I'm sorry to hear that you had a very difficult past. But I have some great news for you."

"What?"

"It's over!" "Your past is over."

In another experience, I wanted to toast our friend on her fortieth birthday, but, in anguish, she declined the toast.

"Don't remind me. I'm the big 4-0!"

"Well, Chrissy," I reasoned, "imagine if this were your sixtieth birthday instead. How much would you give to go back to your fortieth which is where you are right now?"

"Hmm, ok."

"But Chrissy, may I remind you of today when at forty you were upset because you wished you were twenty instead? And I also remember that when you were twenty you were upset because you wanted to be twenty one."

There is only one practical answer. Wherever you are, be there and it will never really matter what age you are. After you either go through a crises or further your practical intelligence, you will realize this insight. Hopefully, it will be the latter.

ARE YOU MAKING THE MISTAKE OF LIMITING THE VISIONS OF YOUR FUTURE BY THE NARROW EXPERIENCES OF YOUR PAST?

Was there a time you weren't toilet trained? Are you toilet trained today? What if you had concluded, "I guess I'll never be toilet trained?"

Was there a time you couldn't read nor write? Can you read and write today? What if you had generalized at that moment in time and concluded, "I guess I'll never be able to read and write?"

Isn't it only logical to assume that some things you couldn't do yesterday can be done today or tomorrow?

How?

By starting to build your future and stopping blaming your past!

TODAY BEGINS YOUR NEW LIFE

Operate out of your practical intelligence and ask yourself, "Isn't today my best chance to change my life?"

Your practical intelligence will start thinking and in a short period of time will rule out both yesterday and tomorrow as being the starting point to the new, unstoppable you. In fact, you can start changing your life by seeing yourself as not a product of your past experiences, but rather as a dream-seed for your future achievements. Start looking forward rather than looking back. Enter this moment, not biased by the weaknesses of your past.

Today you are not your past. Look at a clock or a calendar. Notice that they change every minute and every day. Your body is constantly in change. In fact, it would be impossible to freeze yourself in any given moment in time. Time moves on. In reality, your past is over. Your past cannot touch you today unless you give it power by blaming it.

The only influence that your past has on you is in your perception of your past. Two people who grow up in the same family often have dramatically different views of their family years later because their perceptions are different. It is not our past, but our view of our past that affects us. The person who uses their practical intelligence knows that to change our past, we change our view of our past.

But there is a more effective approach.

- Get off the past.

- Live in the present to

- Build the future

NOW IS OUR ONLY MOMENT OF POWER

Remember, we have about two and one-half billion moments of potential in our life. Imagine that. Two and one-half billion seconds of potential. Any one of those moments could be life changing. Interestingly, a whole life-time looks overwhelming to manage. Our past experiences, our present pressures, our future worries—how do we handle it all?

Relax. We don't have to control our whole life in this moment called "now." All we have to do is to get the most out of this moment. Where we are today is the result of the choices we made in our past moments called "now." Where we will be tomorrow will be the result of the choices we make in this moment "now." Think about it:

How much we weigh at the beginning of next year is related to our choices at mealtime from now until the new year.

Whether or not we get a speeding ticket this year is directly related to our choice of speeding or not.

We play a role in our life. Awareness of our power in this moment called now opens up our world. The problem occurs when we don't use our power by living in our past.

WHAT IS HAPPINESS?
PUTTING YOURSELF INTO
A STATE OF FLOW!

"Flow" is a word used and written about by Mihaly Csikszentmihalyi in his book of the same name. The author concluded that for 2,300 years, since Aristotle asked the question "What is happiness?" no answer could be found. But he argues that we now know what happiness is.

Happiness is the state of being totally absorbed in a task. This is when we are in a flow. Flow improves the quality of that experience and provides increased enjoyment, concentration, and involvement. In flow, the sense of time and self-consciousness disappears and a feeling of transcendence and breaking out of boundaries appears.

Flow is the state of being so absorbed in an activity that nothing else seems to matter. The immersion in the experience itself takes the focus away from self-consciousness and outside problems.

Curiously, happiness is not something that happens nor something that power can command. It does not depend on outside events, but rather on how we interpret them. Happiness is a condition that must be prepared for and cultivated by each of us privately. People who control their inner experiences are those who can determine and enhance the quality of their lives.

PROBLEMS WITH RE-LIVING OUR PAST

As you develop your practical intelligence, it becomes increasingly clear with each lesson that there are many reasons to stop dwelling on the past. Here are three of them. You can add many more.

First, when we focus on the past, we use our power in this now moment with what *was* rather than what *could* be. How many of our moments of potential are lost because of wasting our time on what was. I have a good friend. Ed never knew his biological parents and experienced many setbacks in his young life, but self-determined, Ed consciously moved on. Of course he was curious, and of course, he wanted to meet his parents, but he used his time to build his future, not to blame his past.

A second problem associated with re-living the past is that not only does it consume our finite amount of time, but if we find some answers to why we are the way we are today, how do we know for sure? How can we prove that we are afraid of public speaking because our mother was a perfectionist? And so, what if she were a perfectionist? What should we do, once we gather this "insight?"

Blame our mother? Blame our self? Or move forward?

The third problem with digging up our past, in addition to using up time that could be creating our future and the tenuous nature of our insight, is the fact that we now will start to blame the people and experiences of our past for doing these things to us.

"If it weren't for my past, I could have a great future."

STRATEGIES FOR LEAVING THE PAST BEHIND AND LOOKING FORWARD

Imagine yourself ten years from now talking to yourself today. Think of some current problem you face and ask yourself, that is, your ten-year-older self, "How should I deal with this situation today to make it better for me ten years from now?"

To maximize your life, the ideal is that you are your best in only one moment. And that moment is now. You can't change your past, but you can sure change your future by acting out of who you want to be, not out of who you were. You can begin now by becoming aware of the power of this moment.

THE MOST MOVING INSIGHT OF LIFE

In my practice I constantly wonder why some people suddenly, at some moment of personal transformation, really begin to understand life. Others never experience that illuminating moment that shapes their new future and lifts them up above their past. Interested in the biographies of successful people, I tried to learn why some made it against all odds, while others let the smallest matters send them to live on "The Streets of Past Blames" for the rest of their lives. I thought if we could find the difference, others who were open-minded and ready to grow could benefit. I think we found it.

THE SUCCESS ATTITUDE: FOCUSING ON WHAT CAN BE, NOT ON WHAT WAS

In observing both unhappy (low developed PI) and fulfilled people (high developed PI), there was a major difference between the two in another way. The difference was born in that moment when everything becomes clear about one's relationship with life. What separated the most fulfilled and the least fulfilled humans occurred at the instant they realized that:

> "*I am not an effect of my life experiences (Blame).*"

> "*I am the cause of my life experiences (Live) (High PI).*

Unhappy people inevitably believe that they are an effect, helpless and caused by something over which they have no control, such as their past. The self-actualized person, one who is making more of her possibilities "actual," however, thinks, "I cause. I cause how people see me. I cause how I choose to respond to life. I cause myself to set goals for myself. I cause my future. I face challenges and I cause myself not to give up."

BECOMING A FIND-A-WAYER

The world is divided into two kinds of people. Some give up when faced with a barrier. They make excuses, blame the past or other people, and find fault with everything. One doesn't have to go to the library to learn that this just doesn't work. It's not very practical.

Others, faced with the same challenges, go on to find a way. This works a lot better. Both have the same amount of time — one life time.

Find-a-wayers operate from the conviction that problems have solutions They move from the spirit of Winston Churchill who proclaimed, "If my best isn't good enough, I'll do better!" They draw from their unlimited creative determination to overcome their past views, while others search for rationalizations for their failures.

Please note that rationalization is giving a "good" reason rather than the "true" reason for why we are held back. Explaining that "the sun was in my eyes" appears to be enough reason for an outfielder to miss the ball and lose the game.

On the other hand, a find-a-wayer would have prepared by bringing sunglasses. Rationalizing that one failed to get a promotion because the boss liked someone else better appears to be a good reason, but a find-a-wayer recognizes that it is important to have good human relations skills and tact to gain the boss's trust. The find-a-wayer is aware that all other things being equal, the boss will hire the person with whom they feel most comfortable.

10 RATIONALIZATIONS THAT BLOCK OUR POTENTIAL IN THE PRESENT (PAST WAYS OF LOOKING AT THINGS THAT WE STILL ARGUE ABOUT TODAY)

1. It's never been done before. Or I've never done it before.

2. If only I had this one other thing, I could do the job.

3. The economy is bad.

4. It's my age. I'm not the right age for that.

5. I don't have any luck. I can't get a break.

6. I don't have an educational background in my past.

7. I'm not big enough.

8. I could fail. I tried it before and it didn't work.

9. My health is poor. I'm handicapped.

10 Other people do things like that. Not me.

Let's explore each of these rationalizations and see how they are interpreted differently by find-a-wayers.

1 Instead of the rationalization that "It's never been done before" or "I've never done it before," the find-a-wayer concludes, "I'm not going to limit the visions of my future by the narrow experiences of my past." The find-a-wayer knows that almost everything we see in the world wasn't here at some time and had to be done a first time. In fact, almost everything that you as a human being can do today, you couldn't do in your past. There had to be a first time. The moment that you realize that you are a cause and not an effect, a mental barrier opens up and gives way to a ceilingless sky of potential.

In their popular book, **Mind Power**, Bernie Zilbergeld and Arnold Lazarus wrote:

"Before May 6, 1954, no one had ever run a mile under four minutes; lots of runners had tried and many had come close, but there was a barrier. Many runners and scholars argued that the barrier was physiological, that human bodies simply couldn't run that fast. As Roger Bannister, the first human to break the barrier, said, 'Everyone used to think it was quite impossible and beyond the reach of the runner.' But Bannister never thought this himself and prepared himself accordingly. What is perhaps even more

astonishing than Bannister's own achievement is that once he proved that it could be done, others were also able to do it. By now hundreds and hundreds of runners have run a mile in less than four minutes. It is doubtful that human physiology underwent a significant change in that period. What is far more likely is that before Bannister's accomplishment, the self-limiting notion that the four minute mile was impossible made it impossible. Once Bannister proved it was possible, something changed in the minds of the other runners."

"A similar thing happened in weightlifting. Before Vasily Alexeev lifted 501 pounds in 1976, no one had ever lifted 500 pounds over his head, and many argued that it was a physiological impossibility. But in the month after Alexeev broke the barrier, four other weight lifters lifted over 500 pounds. By now scores have done it. Why? The analysis of Arnold Schwarznegger is undoubtedly correct. 'They believed it was now possible. The body didn't change that month. How could the body change that much? It was the same body, but the mind was different. Mentally it's possible to break records. Once you understand that, you can do it.'"

My friend Leif Cook, the Scandinavian entrepreneur, talks about the impossible this way: "If something is possible, it's already done. If something is impossible, let's begin to do it." Henry

Ford told us, "Believe you can or believe you can't; either way'll you'll be correct." And philosopher Baruch Spinoza urged us mentally over our past when he concluded, "For as long as you believe that something is impossible, for that exact period of time it will be impossible." And we add, "The moment you see that challenge as being reachable, that is the very moment you go on to conquer the challenge."

In speaking to an Ohio graduating class, I asked the cap and gown seniors, "Who in here believes that we can cure the world's hunger problems in the next five years?" Not one of them raised their hands. And I responded, "That's why we won't, because we have already drawn a conclusion in our heads about the impossibility of the challenge. The world needs just one of you in this room to raise your hand to get our hope started. And to stop making the mistake of limiting the visions of our future by the narrow experiences of our past."

2 In lieu of the second rationalization that "if only I had this one other thing, I could succeed," the find-a-wayer looks inside his or her creative mind. A peppy young college girl named Carol Johnston set for herself a goal of becoming a gymnast on a university team. Less than five feet tall, she faced a barrier—she had only one arm. Yet she

didn't spend her time excusing, rationalizing, or blaming. Carol set her will compass on a course for success and worked harder. The petite mountain of inspiration concluded that having only one arm meant she had to find a way by working harder than anyone else. Her mind made up for what was missing in her body.

Competing against hundreds of other girls with both arms, she made the UCLA gymnastic team. Her success story did not end there. Carol became one of the top gymnasts in the world! Often the only missing part for finding the way to our dreams is in our mind.

3 The rationalization that "I can't succeed because of the economy" is inferior to the view that "I, not the economy, decide my next move." In his important book, *The Magic of Getting What You Want*, Davis Schwartz wrote, "Huge, prosperous businesses such as McDonalds, Ford, Kentucky Fried Chicken were started by people with very little capitol. Furthermore, all except for two of the people who led the United States, Hoover, Truman, Eisenhower, Johnson, Nixon, Ford, Carter, Reagan, and Clinton were born to poor or moderately well-off parents.

Often the economy doesn't destroy a business, but the attitudes that people develop about a downhill economy lead them to act in ways to cause defeat and create a self-fulfilling prophecy of failure. A friend of mine had a successful sandwich shop in a small Pennsylvania town. In addition to the economy slipping at the time, a big restaurant opened across the street. My friend was defeated in his mind weeks before the other restaurant opened its door. When the restaurant finally opened, in a short while he was telling me about the customers he was losing. They were going "across the street." As we talked, he began to realize how his defeatist attitude was causing his business failure.

"You see, Lew, I knew the economy was getting bad and then that new restaurant opened. So I immediately started cutting back on orders to prepare for the slowdown. For the last few days, in fact, I haven't had any bread or rolls left for sandwiches in the evening. As you can suspect, even some of my regulars started going over there because I couldn't give them what they wanted."

I asked my gloomy friend, "Wait a second. Are you saying that you cut back in orders because somehow or other you knew that your competition would take away your regulars? And while they were still coming to you, you couldn't serve them so that they had to go across the street?"

"Yes."

Grayson County Public Library
Independence, VA

"Well, perhaps that suggests that you better take a clearer look at your future in a more positive way and increase your orders so that a customer will never have to leave disappointed. Perhaps now, in this economy, is the time to start offering specials and taking advantage of all the new traffic that your competition is bringing into the area. Don't defeat yourself by blaming the economy. Let the economy, whether it be positive or negative, work in your favor. Don't accept the rationalization of the economy."

To a find-a-wayer, ideas and creativity are more important than money. The only value of money is that it enables you to find and hire find-a-wayers.

4 Find-a-wayers don't lean on the excuse of age and reject the "I'm not the right age" rationalization. Can you imagine someone finding a cure for a common cold and having people with colds asking the question, "How old is the discoverer?" Age is a rationalization that blocks the go forward spirit. Theodore Roosevelt, John Kennedy, and Bill Clinton were in their early 40s when they became a President of the United States. Dwight Gooden was 20 when he was the best pitcher in baseball. Michael Dell was in fourth grade when he applied to take his high school equivalency test. Numerous high tech businesses were built

by entrepreneurs who became millionaires in their early 20s.

By the same token, "too old" has been another historic excuse for not trying. As I watched Grandma Hilda on TV at age 92, on top of Japan's largest mountain, and heard her say, "This sort of climb keeps you young," my eyes were opened to the possibilities of an inspired human at any age. Colonel Sanders founded Kentucky Fried Chicken after he had retired.

David Schwartz puts the question of being too old in real perspective in his book, *The Magic of Thinking Big*. After a training session, a man told Dr. Schwartz that he was thinking of a career change, but he would have to start from scratch. At his age of 40, it would be quite difficult. Schwartz asked the man when he thought a person's productive years began. They agreed at around age 20. They also agreed that even very conservatively speaking, one's productive years end at age 70. Schwartz pointed out that there are 50 years of productivity in a person's life. The man, at age 40, had used up only 20 of his 50 years. He still had 30 years or 60 per cent of his productive years left. And he was afraid of making a change!

Psychiatrist Alfred Adler was once told by a middle-aged person, "I'm too old to go to school because if I start today, it will be four years until

I earn the degree." Adler responded, "And, if you start tomorrow, it will be four years and a day."

It is the rare person who, underneath, doesn't harbor the excuse of inappropriate age. How many people actually do feel they are at just the right age? What is the right age?

Any age is right, and no age is more right than the age you are ... today. You have never had so much experience and you will never be younger than you are today!

5   Instead of the rationalization that "I don't have any luck" or "I can't get a break," find-a-wayers don't wait for breaks and luck. They believe that highly motivated, persistent people attract good luck and get the breaks. While writing a book, **Think Your Way To Success**, I did some research to uncover whether there was a difference between the ways successful and unsuccessful people viewed the role of luck in their lives. I encourage you to try the same experiment.

First, identify five people in your life who you consider happy and successful. Then compose a list of five people whom you consider less than successful and down on life. Ask all ten people the same question.

Ask the people in your survey: "How much of a role do you believe luck plays in your life? Then record all ten answers so that you can scientifically analyze patterns in their responses, if any. If you find that the five you identified as successful have a different pattern in their responses from the other five, you may have discovered a view that has a huge consequence on success.

Until you obtain your results, allow me to share some of the responses I received from my interviews. First, the unhappy group:

"Luck is everything. You just have to be at the right place, at right time." (Male, age 27, unemployed for three and one-half years. He has not filled out a job application for two years and lives with his parents.)

"The cards of life are stacked against you if you don't have money." (Female, 36, former sales woman who recently lost her position because of poor sales performance and missed appointments)

"Some people just get all of the breaks in life." (Male 19, recent college dropout)

As you analyze these three responses, you'll notice that each gives luck the key role in determining success. They just were not lucky, and didn't get the breaks, have the money, or know the right people.

Next, here are some responses that I classified as happy, successful and in charge of their lives.

"You make your own luck." (Female, age 32, recently received an award for being one of the top ten teachers in the State of Pennsylvania)

"It wasn't luck that I haven't missed a single sales appointment in the last two years. It wasn't luck that I made sure that every single order I received from customers was promptly filled. It wasn't luck that I made it my business to take at least four sales training or motivation courses every year. It wasn't luck that I went back to school in the evenings and in less than eight years earned a bachelor's degree in business. Come to think of it, it wasn't luck that my shoes were shined and my shirts were spotless when I made my sales calls. No, it wasn't luck that made me the top salesman last year. And, it won't be luck when I do it again this year." (Male, 39, top salesman)

My favorite response came from an author of fiction books. He described how early in life he was discouraged from a career in writing by failure-centered thinkers who told him it was impossible to get a book published unless you either had a lot of money or an "in." His response to the question asking his thoughts on the role of luck on success was:

"I concluded that waiting for luck to come to me before I did something myself was like looking into the mirror at my reflection and waiting for my reflection to move first. There is a more effective way. When I move, my reflection will passively follow. Everytime."

The attitudes of successes and failures became clear to me, and, I trust, will become clear to you when you analyze the results of your interviews. Failures tend to believe that people become successful because of things outside themselves. Thus, they wait, wish and hope for a break. And then, when it doesn't come, they rationalize, excuse and blame.

Successful people, contrarily, tend to see achievement as a product of personal effort. And, if there is such a thing as luck, then highly motivated, persistent people are the ones who, in the long run, tend to attract it. As one philosopher concluded, "The best winds seem to favor the best sailors."

6 While rationalizers stop themselves from forward progress because of not having the right "background," find-a-wayers believe the "backbone is more important than the background." Rationalizers look into the past to see what is missing and give up because of it. A find-a-wayer's view of

the same situation is, "I am determined to learn whatever I need to learn to reach my goal. I may have to work a little harder because I don't have the formal background, but that doesn't matter. With determination, I will compensate."

President Truman, regarded by some as one of the gutsier U.S. Presidents, might not have run for the highest office in the land because he had a only a high school education. That didn't stop him and he learned what he had to learn to get the presidency.

Albert Einstein, rather than giving up after failing physics, plowed forward to learn everything he could on his own. His insights changed the world, and it is the physics understood by Einstein that the world now studies.

Thomas Edison, perhaps the greatest inventor the world has known, quit school at age 8. He sold newspapers on a street corner, and by age 9 had sub-contracted his paper route to a younger child so that he could spend each day in the Detroit Library. The light bulb, phonograph, curling iron, and synthetic rubber are just a few of his more than 1,000 inventions.

My friend Ed Rose enjoyed going to the great annual, highly informative conference conducted by The University of North Texas Center for the Study of Work Teams. He had a message to deliver.

He was asked if he was a university graduate and if he had written any books like the other presenters had. He did neither, but his heart guaranteed that Ed's future would be brighter than his past. He enrolled at a Florida university, wrote a half dozen books, and like magic, you can now see him passionately conducting a workshop at the September Conference. Ed is also the Worldwide Training Manager of the huge Intersil Corporation. Don't tell Ed your background is holding you back unless you are ready for a twenty-four hour motivational session.

Another good buddy, and my personal role model, is Tom Chlebos, one of the leaders at S.C. Johnson Wax who helped transform the great family-owned company into a work team environment. It's a tough job to change the way people work. But Tom and his team learned everything they could about teams, and through his winning personality and his knowledge, today the company steeped in a hundred-year philosophy of believing in people is truly living its dream. And, in his modest way, Tom, sitting in the background, spends his time giving credit to others. Tom had to learn all about teams and today he is one of the leading experts in the world on creating a team-based work environment.

Avoid the rationalization of not initially having the background knowledge and remember the examples of Truman, Einstein, Edison, Ed Rose, and Tom Chlebos. Simply become determined to learn everything you need to know to reach your dream. The library door of life is always open for the determined person.

7 The "I'm not big enough" rationalization is easily overcome with the realization that "physical size is one thing, but visionary stature is another, related only to the depths of one's mind." Find-a-wayers don't let their current size affect who they will be in the future.

In the early 1900s, the National Football League was founded. A little city called Green Bay, Wisconsin formed a team. The city had less than 20,000 people, but its size in thinking was equal to New York, Boston, and Chicago. By 1957, the team had moved from playing in the high school to a stadium with 58,000 seats for a population of only 63,000. Big thinking. Every game was sold out, and a few years later the little city of Green Bay proudly won its first Super Bowl game.

At five feet, five inches, Spud Webb is the shortest basketball player in the pro's, and he can dunk a basketball. Size of vision is what counts. Don't be intimidated by the big competitors. Think big. And, remember, size is related to just one thing: the depth of the vision in your mind.

There will never be a better time for you than right now!

8 Rationalizers don't act because they are afraid they might fail. Find-a-wayers believe that one fails only by failing to act. Find-a-wayers believe that "I could never fail because no matter what happens when I act, I get knowledge, feedback, and information that makes me better equipped for the future."

Remember, you cannot fail. When you act, you receive knowledge, feedback, and results. When you fail to act, you fail to get information you can use for your future.

9 Rationalizing that "my health is poor, so I can't succeed" gives way to the find-a-wayer's conviction that "although my health may not allow me to do some things, that doesn't mean I can't do anything. There are many things I can do and I will excel at them."

I'll never forget an incident that happened a few years ago when handicapped children were getting on a school bus for the first day of school. A helpful woman tried to assist a teenager up the steps. Politely, he turned to her and said, "Thanks anyway, but I can see and I can walk. I have a

hearing problem, but everything else I can do."
The kind woman made the mistake of generaliz-
ing from a single problem to a general problem.

We all tend to make the same mistakes at
times, thinking that because we can't do one
thing as a result of health issues, we can't do anything at all. Nothing could be farther from the
truth.

President Eisenhower and Johnson had heart
attacks, as has Vice President Cheney, but that
didn't stop them from reaching for their dreams.

Helen Keller inspired us that "one cannot con-
sent to creep when one has the impulse to soar."

Ray Charles and Stevie Wonder learned to see
with their fingers, their ears, and their hearts.
Stevie Wonder even wrote a song describing the
birth of his little girl: *"Isn't She lovely?"*

10

Rationalizers think that other people, not
people like them, do great things. Find-a-
wayers know that "great things are
achieved by humans, just like me, who have an
extraordinary determination to surmount any
obstacle and the creative determination to find a
way." Remember: most people make two mistakes, overestimating others and underestimating
themselves.

The truth is that when you lift your chin in determination, and you have a passionate purpose in life, you have what you need.

LIVE TODAY: USE THIS MOMENT AS AN END IN ITSELF

Imagine: some students take college courses to get a degree, to graduate, to get a good job, to retire early. Most of our lives we are doing something now because it will lead to a reward that we will receive later. When you think about it then, most of our valuable two and one-half billion moments of life are lost and consumed as mere moments to serve another end. Another moment later, sometime in the future, will be the rewarding one.

When we are living this powerful moment called now fully, we are creating more rewarding moments for ourself. The college student taking the science course who puts his heart into the course and "flows," enjoys today's course as an end in itself—not as a means to a good grade.

IT DOESN'T MATTER WHERE YOU HAVE BEEN. IT ONLY MATTERS WHERE YOU ARE GOING

No one has a perfect past. Everyone has had a problem with this or that. The rich look back and experience their loss of privacy and their distrust of being valued for their money, rather than for themselves. The poor focus on all the things they didn't have. Everyone has a strong argument to feel shorted. This book is not designed to further those arguments, but to say that the most practical thing that we can do—rich or poor, privileged or deprived—is to move ourselves forward.

The answer never lies in what was, but rather in what will be. Get the momentum started in your own life. Build your practical intelligence and go forward. Tomorrow you will be farther than you are today. See what's right with you, rather than what's wrong with you. That is the way to look at things because that will make your future brighter, and fill up your present with possibilities.

3

POSITIVE FOCUSING

*Strengthens More Than Blaming
Our Weaknesses*

WE SEE MORE OF WHATEVER
WE FOCUS ON

The next time you are in a room full of people, pick a color that you see in the room. For example, imagine that you choose the color red. Look more closely around you and try to isolate everything that is red. Red sweaters, dresses, ties, carpets, drapes, Coke cans, etc. Take a minute or so and bring everything red into the foreground by focusing on red.

You soon will notice things that are red that you didn't notice before. The red may even appear like it is reaching out to you. Maybe the room even looks like it is dominated by red things. Every other color starts to become insignificant, just blending into the background.

Now, close your eyes and erase your red focusing. When you open your eyes again, choose another color to give your perceptual power away to.

Focus on white. Bring everything white strongly into the foreground. Soon you will see more white than you ever dreamed was in the room. Slowly, red and all of the other colors will fade into the background.

One of the fastest ways to change your world is to change your focus. What you focus on, you begin to see more of.

SEE NEGATIVES IN PERSPECTIVE

While in a taxi en route to a speaking engagement to students in an Omaha school, I told the driver I was going to be working with teenagers.

Bitter, he argued, "Teenagers, I'll tell you about teenagers."

He pulled out the Omaha newspaper and threw the headlines to me.

"Look at that!"

"Two Omaha Boys Caught Starting a Warehouse Fire," the headlines read.

"That's what we have in teenagers!" he added.

I asked him how many teenagers there were in all of Omaha.

Obviously uninformed, he replied, "About 40,000."

"Wow," I returned, "if I were the editor of today's newspaper, the headlines would have read, "Rejoice— 39,998 or 99.99+% of Omaha Children Not Caught Starting Warehouse Fires!"

What do you want to build your own life philosophy on—the 39,998 or the 2? While both are facts, which one is more common? Obviously, there are many times more children who are responsible. Both newspapers and many, everyday conversations focus on the rare—which is the negative.

Once we decide to focus on what's right or what's wrong, we will immediately begin seeing more of what we chose to look for. And obviously, you can see the tremendous advantage an optimist has over a pessimist. They both see whatever they look for.

THE DIFFERENCE BETWEEN BLAMING OURSELVES AND TAKING RESPONSIBILITY

Once we stop blaming others, instead of judging them, we will sensitively listen to them to understand them more effectively from their vantage point. And, in the process, we are not blaming ourselves or blaming others. In other words, we take responsibility to change our behavior, not to blame ourselves ("If it weren't for me being a blamer, we could get along!")

Or, when we take responsibility for our life today, rather than living in the past, we move forward without blame. Blaming is unproductive and has the accompanying thought, "If it weren't for me being so rotten and dwelling on the past, I could get ahead. It's all my fault."

In blaming, we actually blame ourselves for holding ourselves back. "We could be so much better if it weren't for ourselves!"

Self-blamers put the blame for their behavior on themselves rather than holding themselves responsible. When people take the blame for their behavior, it is just as unproductive as placing the blame on external factors. Blame is a moral judgment and tends to a lead to a negative personal evaluation, but no change in actions.

Taking responsibility, rather than self-blaming is more productive. When people take personal responsibility, they act courageously and are not immobilized by their own feelings of worthlessness. But self-blamers are so filled with blame, guilt, shame, and doubt that they use all of their energies blaming themselves and have no energies left to get out of their self-created ruts. So, whereas self-blame results in self-pity, personal responsibility results in action and change.

Self-blamers, in a curious way, have a real luxury. After all, if they feel guilty, they don't have to change! Surely just feeling guilty is suffering enough, they reason. If they feel weak, then surely someone strong will come along and take on their responsibilities.

Self-blamers wallow in rejection. They feel that their worth has been attacked and they choose immobility. Self-responsible, courageous people are more concerned about increasing their skills. Self-responsible people learn from situations. They use their energies to develop a more constructive plan rather than to swim in self-defeating emotions. They are active and responsible, whereas self-blamers are passive and irresponsible.

TAKE TODAY TO REALIZE
WHAT IS RIGHT WITH YOU

Most people are more talented at seeing their shortcomings than they are at seeing their assets, strengths, resources, and potential. They don't realize that if they have strengths and don't acknowledge those positive qualities, they are fooling themselves. Don't lie to yourself. The world needs you to be your best—to be what is already right about you.

Sit back for a few minutes, play some relaxing music or go to a peaceful setting, and ask yourself each of the following ten questions. After brainstorming with yourself after each question, jot down your impressions on a piece of paper to keep for the rest of your life.

1 What are some things I accomplished that have given me personal satisfaction?

Some areas you might include are:

- school accomplishments, including particular subjects

- social accomplishments, such as helping a friend through a tough time or inspiring someone to believe in herself

- parental achievements

- athletic achievement

- personal challenges

- physical successes, such as losing weight

- professional successes

- spiritual development

Think about these things in time lines:

Ages

0-9 _____

_____

_____

10-19 _____

_____

_____

20-29 _____

_____

_____

30-39 _____

_____

_____

40-49 _____

_____

_____

50-59 _____

_____

_____

60-69 _____

_____

_____

70+ _____

_____

_____

2

What do I consider to be my 5 most important assets? (Don't move on until you have listed at least 5.)

a. _____
_____
_____

b. _____
_____
_____

c. _____
_____
_____

d. _____
_____
_____

e. _____
_____
_____

3

Who are 5 people that I respect most in the world.
What do I have in common with each of them?

a. _____
_____
_____

b. _____
_____
_____

c. _____
_____
_____

d. _____
_____
_____

e. _____
_____
_____

4

What are 5 things I have done for other people that were really helpful to them at the time?

a. _____

_____

_____

b. _____

_____

_____

c. _____

_____

_____

d. _____

_____

_____

e. _____

_____

_____

5

What are the 3 best qualities I have that I can give in a personal relationship?

a. _____
_____
_____

b. _____
_____
_____

c. _____
_____
_____

6 Who would really get a boost today from a surprise call from me?

_____

_____

_____

_____

7 What is the thing in my life that I wanted the most, worked hard at, and finally achieved? Recall the experience, and then list the 3 top positive qualities it took for you to achieve that goal.

a. _____

_____

_____

b. _____

_____

_____

c. _____

_____

_____

8 When did I fail at something and then, with my determination, fight back and overcome the failure? As you relive the experience, what are the 2 most important qualities you needed to come back?

a. _____
   _____
   _____

b. _____
   _____
   _____

9 Is there a time when my attitude was the difference in a situation? Remember the situation and recall talking to your attitude. What did you tell your attitude that eventually changed it and helped you through the situation?

_____
_____
_____
_____
_____

10

What trait would I like to develop today? Go over the list of the previous 9 questions, gain strength from it, and ask your attitude to help bring out this trait that you desire because it is inside you.

_____

_____

_____

_____

_____

GETTING ENTHUSED ABOUT YOURSELF AND YOUR UNIQUENESS

You are literally a miracle. You are such a rare combination of the physical and spiritual that there is no one, anywhere in the world, exactly like you. You are so special that you have been given the greatest gift in the world. You were selected to be a human being. You are the owner of your body, your mind, your actions, your thoughts, your feelings, and your attitude. Even your dreams are uniquely yours. And this is your moment in the history of our universe. You are alive, and this gives you the power to draw up the blueprints for the kind of person you want to be.

Tap the human powers you have by igniting the power of enthusiasm for yourself and your possibilities. In fact, you are your possibilities in the beginning stages just waiting to happen. Your success happens when you focus a light on what's right with you. You can start by becoming enthusiastic and let it show.

To become enthusiastic:

Smile enthusiastically. Wherever you go, watch the life-giving power your smile has on people. Ask people the question, "Who would you rather be with, an enthusiastic person or a person with a frown?" It's a surprise to you, I'm sure, that not one single person chose the frown. Be the energy wherever you go. Even if it seems unnatural to first extend a warm, welcoming smile to everyone, it will soon be as natural to you as tying your shoes. To realize the power of a smile, just think of two people.

The first person, who never smiles, we'll call I. M. Dull. How do you feel around I. M. Dull? Would you be likely to buy something from I. M. Dull? Would you enjoy listening to I. M. Dull?

Now consider another person—a good listener who meets you with a warm smile. Let's call this person N. Thusiastic. N. Thusiastic listens to you, gets excited about the things that interest you, and is very respectful and positive. Doesn't this person give you more life than I. M. Dull? Be determined that you will use your self-determined resource, your attitude, and translate your positive attitude to your life and go forward in the world with a big smile. It will give you a huge advantage.

Walk enthusiastically. Enthusiasts walk faster. Why not? They are going places. Compare the walks of I. M. Dull and N. Thusiastic. While Dull walks with his head down, shoulders curved inward, and with a short, apologetic step, N. Thusiastic walks with his head up (even in the rain), shoulders back, and has crisp gait. Without even meeting these two people, you draw conclusions about them, just by observing their walks. Their walks tell a story. Interestingly, research demonstrates that most of the victims of muggings tend to have a certain walk. Prisoners who were serving time for muggings agreed that a person's walk strongly influenced their decision to attack. The person most likely to become a mugging victim takes short, shuffling steps with their chest buried between their shoulders. Remember, your walk stems from your self-image, but your self-image can be enhanced from how you walk. Change the way you walk, like N. Thusiast, and soon the world will see that you are going places, but more importantly, you will feel yourself getting places faster. Win people over even before you meet them by your confident, enthusiastic walk.

Get psyched on yourself by speaking enthusiastically. Modulate your voice. Every person can remember never-ending church sermons given by a monotonous speaker. Yet, the same words brought to life by an enthusiastic speaker can give energy to the group and make the sermon even more powerful. You remember teachers, as well, who brought their lessons to life. Or perhaps you have experienced a sales person who went on to simply describe a house, a car, or even furniture with no life. The enthusiast puts vitality in the talk. Hold people's attention by putting refreshment in everything you say. Say "hello!' with meaning. Say "congratulations" with a thrill. Say "have a great day!" with belief and enthusiasm.

When you vitalize things, something interesting happens. You actually invigorate yourself. When someone asks you how you are doing, do you just say "OK" or even more helplessly, "awful," or do you respond with an energetic "I'm turbo charged!" By enlivening your responses, you are lifted. Remember: your words are emotional triggers to your attitude. Watch what you say.

Never say anything that you don't want to be realized. Remember, you are the director of your attitude tools— your thoughts, your emotions, and your actions. When you put yourself down, your attitude follows your advice:

"I never did well in a math class."

"I'm no good at selling."

Your attitude is your servant. And when you steer it into a negative direction, it will go and use its massive resources of thoughts, emotions, and actions and bring you back the results you requested.

That is why speaking enthusiastically and telling yourself things like "this is going to be a great day" trigger your attitude to use its tools to make the day positive for you.

Use a vocabulary filled with enthusiastic words. More and more psychological research demonstrates the power of words on a person's emotions. When you think about it, down-and-out people tend to have a vocabulary filled with gloomy, inactive, and depressing words. On the other hand, enthusiastic people tend to use words that overflow with positive, uplifting, active, and, if need be, assertive words. Two prominent behavioral scientists, Albert Ellis and Robert Harper, co-authors of *A New Guide to Rational Living*, and Charles Zastrow, author of *Talk to Yourself*, demonstrate how we create our emotions by the words we use. Uplift your life by using uplifting words.

Compare the Words of Our Friends
I. M. Dull and N. Thusiastic:

Failure vs. Success Vocabulary

I. M. Dulls says	N. Thusiastic says
"Things are awful, terrible."	"We face an exciting challenge."
"I hate aging."	"I love aging. Consider the option."
"I'm too old to change."	"My experiences give me an advantage."
"Maybe it can be done."	"Knowing us, we can do it."
"Things are OK."	"Things are great."
"Let's give up. It's no use."	"Let's put ourselves into second gear."
"Good job."	"Fantastic performance."

Like N. Thusiast, build yourself on a foundation of strong, positive words. If you do, you'll notice your emotions change before your very own eyes. And more importantly, you will be realizing your tremendous power to direct and control your attitude—which means your life.

Wake up enthusiastically. In the morning, while most people treat their alarm clocks like their enemy, look at your alarm clock as though it were a friendly fire alarm. When it rings, jump out of bed fired up with enthusiasm. Put an immediate, early morning glow in your mind and in your heart. An enthusiastic start to the day gives you an advantage over the ho-hum person who needs an hour, or a morning cup of coffee, or a morning smoke to get going.

Answer your telephone enthusiastically. Get off automatic pilot and get enthused every time your telephone rings. Remember, the person has taken the time to call you. Let the person catch your enthusiasm right from the start. While the programmed robot says a dull hello, the enthusiast answers with a cheery "Good morning" or even "With a little good news from you, both of our days can be even better!"

Your opening words on the telephone are only limited by your creativity!

Listen enthusiastically. Win people over by employing the rarely used skill of enthusiastic listening. As you listen to people talk, lean forward. Use open, expressive eyes conveying full attention to the speaker's ideas. The world's best sales people are not only great speakers, but enthusiastic listeners, as well. Stay away from playing games like "I can top that" when listening to another share a proud achievement.

In addition to using your enthusiasm (because it works better than apathy), you can increase your practical intelligence by empowering yourself by drawing from the bigger you.

ACT OUT OF YOUR UNLIMITED SPIRIT, NOT YOUR DEFENSIVE EGO

You can put your radio on either AM or FM. Your choice will affect what you hear.

In your everyday life, you can make a similar choice, to either act out of your defensive ego or out of your unlimited spirit. Our ego is our smallest possible self and gives us very little strength and power to cope with our life challenges. When we act out of our unlimited spirit, we are operating out of our creative resources, as wide as the universe of our minds.

Let's compare the relative capacity, force, and vitality present in each of the two extremes.

Ego State	Spirit State
Self-blaming	Inspirational
Threatened	Embraces

Physical Form	Boundless Energies
Limited in Time	Timeless Reference
Limited in Place	Universal
Defends	Creates
Maintenance	Enhancement
Disease Mentality	Wellness, Potential Model
Fatigues	Regenerates
Self-conscious	Spontaneous
Doubts or believes	Knows
Restricts	Empowers
Takes, Consumes	Gives, Creates
Hesitates	Flows
Moment as means to end	Moment as end in itself

Picture the ego as closing you up, while the spirit opens you up to new resources within yourself—the universe in your mind and heart. Consider just a few of the major changes that occur when you transform yourself from an ego to a spirit mode. It's even more powerful than changing your radio from AM to FM.

1. Transforming myself from self-blaming ego to inspiration spirit produces in me a sensation of not judging myself, but rather inspiring myself.

2. Transforming myself from being threatened by outside forces to embracing and incorporating those outside forces allows me to absorb and grow from an experience, rather than close myself off from it because of being threatened.

3. Transforming myself from physical form to boundless energy gives me the realization that I am more than my body and my physical possessions. I will live on long after my physical body withers away, just as those whose energies have touched my life live on in my spirit even after their body forms leave. If something can move something or someone else, it is proof of its existence.

4. Transforming myself from the boundaries of this moment in time to a timeless reference point allows me to draw resources, strengths and insights from a universal time perspective.

5. Transforming myself and my thinking from this limited vantage point, this neighborhood place, to a new vantage point, the universe, I gain resources I was never aware of before. Yet, I can do this without leaving my neighborhood. I don't have to go somewhere else in the world to understand. I only have to go somewhere else in my world to understand. The universe is within.

6. Transforming myself from defending my closed-up ego to creating from my opened-up spirit expands me to as large as my universal mind.

7. Transforming my ego from a maintenance, protective mode to an enhancement mode enlarges me and grows me to actualize, not just survive.

8. Transforming myself from a disease mentality (what's wrong here?) to a wellness and spiritual, potential model (what's possible here?) changes my focus and the very questions I ask myself in life.

9. Transforming my ego, which gets fatigued under stress, to mobilizing my universal resources to regenerate my energies renews rather than fatigues me.

10. Transforming my self-conscious ego to become universally aware takes the pressure off my efforts and performance. I'm too busy creating out of my spontaneity to notice and judge myself.

11. Transforming myself from doubting to knowing gives me the certainty to move forward.

12. Transforming myself from physical restrictions because of my limited physical ego to empowering myself with deeper powers enlarges my awareness of my already-there universe.

13. Transforming myself from a taking or consuming motivation to nourish and feed my ego, to a giving and creating motivation enables me to feel my impact on the external world.

14. Transforming myself from a hesitation state to a "flow" mode allows me to get more out of each moment.

15. Transforming myself from using this moment as a means to an end to using it as an end in itself enables me to find rewards now, not to wait until later.

LOOK UP OR LOOK DOWN: CHOOSE WHICH WAY YOU WANT TO GO!

Practical intelligence tells us that we see more of whatever we focus on.

We can focus on all the things that we don't have. When we choose to look down, we will immediately begin seeing even more and more of those things that we were deprived of. Then we can blame life. And we will start building even a stronger case for how we are persecuted.

Or, we can look up. We can see our abundance. We are alive. We have love in our lives. Five and one half of the six billion people in the world would probably change places with us. This is our moment in the history of a magnificent universe. What can we become if we don't look back to who we were?

Which is the intelligent approach to your future: dwelling on blaming your past or using your unlimited mind to build your future?

And which will be more intelligent: to begin tomorrow or to start today?

See how simple this is becoming? You're getting smarter.

Let's make it last by building your future by making your attitude less dependent upon outside things. That way, we can be fairly sure you are going to keep going.

4

INNER CONFIDENCE

Lasts Longer Than Outer
Dependency

Your future is up to one of two things: either (1) you or (2) something else outside of you (luck, fate, superstition, the stars, the environment, etc.)

HOW DEPENDENT ARE YOU ON YOUR ENVIRONMENT?

What would you do, if, from this moment onward, for the rest of your life, no one ever again approved of your actions, applauded you, told you how great you looked, or said, "Good job!"

Would you still survive? Would you start to doubt yourself? Would you go crazy for approval? Would you be weaker and less secure ten years from now?

Or would you start gaining strength from within and keep going forward, driven by your own inner knowing? Would you start realizing that others are probably also so busy being caught up in waiting for approval from others that they don't have time to approve of you? Wouldn't it be vital and important for you to develop your own inner confidence? Inner confidence is inner security. Your only true security is inside you. Because you will always have you!

THE PERSONAL GROWTH JOURNEY: GOING FROM EXTRINSIC TO INTRINSIC MOTIVATION

We are **ex**trinsically motivated when our behavior is determined by external sources, like praise from others or fear of punishment from outside sources. So when our reason for motivation is outside of us, we need to be pushed or pulled, praised or punished, from our environment. We give our environment the power. This is when we also, consequently, blame our environment for not giving us a pat on the back. When our outside source of motivation is not present, our motivation fades.

When we are extrinsically motivated, we never know how good our day is going to be because we don't know whether people will praise us today or not.

We are motivated by **in**trinsic factors when we are driven from within. Pride, joy in achievement, the desire for creativity, and the feeling of satisfaction from a job well done are all products of intrinsic motivation. Do you remember times when you wanted to achieve something so much, just for the excitement you felt inside you? You, at those times, were being pushed by the truest forces of motivation. Yours. This is practical intelligence because you are with yourself practically all of the time.

When our security foundation is inside us, we are driven by inner forces, and we function just as effectively when we receive reinforcement from without as when we don't. And when our security is within, we have an internal point of evaluation and can correct and reinforce ourselves.

In his book, **Flow**, Mihaly Csikszentmihalyi recorded the insights he gained from his study of the healthiest humans. On the subject of inner security versus environmental dependency, he encouraged humans to draw from within. This is what the healthiest humans do. Commenting on the paradox that, despite our technological advancement today, we feel more helpless than our ancestors, the author writes:

> *"There is no way out of the predicament than for the individual to take things in hand personally. If values and institutions no longer*

provide a framework as they once did, each person must use whatever tools are available to carve out a meaningful, enjoyable life ..."

"To overcome the anxieties and depressions of contemporary life, individuals must become independent of their social environment to the degree that they no longer respond exclusively in terms of its rewards and punishments. To achieve such an autonomy, a person has to learn to provide rewards to herself. She has to develop the ability to find enjoyment and purpose, regardless of external circumstances."

The greatest gift that you can give yourself is to trust yourself and keep yourself going and going toward your own self-determined dreams, fueled by your own inner sources. You always have you.

DEVELOPING INNER SECURITY STARTS THE PROCESS OF BECOMING A PERSON

In his book **On Becoming a Person**, Carl Rogers described the direction a person starts to take when moving toward inner security and intrinsic motivation. Rogers writes:

"The individual increasingly comes to feel that the locus of evaluation lies within himself. Less and less does he look to others for

approval or disapproval; for external stan-
dards to live by for decisions and choices. He
recognizes it rests within himself to choose.
And the question which matters is, 'Am I liv-
ing in a way which is deeply satisfying to me,
and in a way which truly expresses me.'"

And when you feel alone in the process of becoming your greater self, and the outside world isn't applauding, be aware that you are not alone. All success stories are about people who have taken the journey of inner trust, strength, and inner support. Rogers writes:

"El Greco must have realized as he looked at
some of his early art work that 'other artists
don't paint that way.' But, somehow or other
he trusted his own inner experiencing of life,
the process of himself, sufficiently that he
could go on expressing his own unique per-
ceptions. It was as though he could say,
'Good artists don't paint like this. But I paint
like this.'"

"Einstein seems to have been unusually
oblivious to the fact that good physicists do
not think his kind of thoughts. Rather than
drawing back on an inadequate preparation
in physics, he simply moved toward being
Einstein, toward thinking his own thoughts,
toward being as truly himself as he could.
This is not a phenomenon which occurs only

*in the artist and genius. Time and again, in
my clients, I have seen simple people become
significant and creative in their own spheres,
as they developed more trust of the process
going on within themselves, and have dared
to feel their own feelings, and express themselves in their own unique way."*

Remember the theme of this book, "If it weren't for ...,
I could be ...!" What we blame, we give our power to.
Whatever I wait for to keep me motivated, the longer I wait.
And if the outside source doesn't motivate me, I spend my
energies blaming, rather than pulling from within and creating my own path to my self-determined dream. Consider
a personal example of the power of inner security, intrinsic
motivation, and a positive self-image.

ROSE AND CHARLES

One of the most moving experiences I ever had occurred
while I was Director of Admissions for an eastern
Pennsylvania college. One day, a 29-year-old woman with
cerebral palsy arrived at our admissions office door in her
wheelchair. Her goal was to attend college. Our interview
with her was still in its initial stages when it became obvious that the girl's very serious speech problem made it
impossible for a meaningful dialogue to take place. She had
to repeat every phrase at least four or five times before we
were able to intelligibly connect her utterances. When time
and again we failed to understand her words, Rose's head

would bend to the side, her face assuming grimaces that reflected her frustration. Patiently she would regroup her energies to try and speak again.

Not only did she lack an ability to effectively speak, the young woman could barely read and she could not write at all. She was truly deficient in most of the key skills necessary to achieve success in college. But in spite of all the odds, "something inside" brought Rose to our admissions office with the goal of becoming a college graduate.

Rose was apparently unaware that the college was unequipped to serve her special needs. Unable to walk without assistance, how could she make it up the steps to the classrooms on the second floor? Lacking the fine coordination to write, how could she take notes? How would she be tested? Which professors would be willing to admit her to their classrooms and face the many burdens and frustrations of dealing with her many special needs? Every thought that could sift though a narrow person's mind seemed to point directly to the conclusion that Rose was not college material and that the college was not prepared to help her climb her ladder of success.

Rose, however, had one asset that helped her soar over all of those mountains of obstacles. That singular but paramount asset was her belief that she could succeed. She had a positive self-image, the key ingredient in the recipe for success. Her self-image, and positive attitude that it gave birth to, impressed the college admissions staff so much that she was given the green light to attend. After Rose was granted admission to the college, a strange thing happened:

people at the college began to believe in Rose and, by believings, they started to find solutions to deal with each of the barriers, one by one. One administrator even commented that he had seen hundreds of students with above average intelligence who did not succeed in college because they lacked what Rose possessed—a positive self-image and a belief that she could succeed. (Allow me to ask you whether you would prefer a brand new automobile in the middle of a desert with no gas in it or an older car with a full tank of fuel? Or would you rather have nothing at all but a tremendous belief in and enthusiasm about yourself or have everything with no hope or self-confidence at all?) Rose had a full tank of enthusiasm, hope, and confidence! She enthusiastically began her college career. Not long after Rose was admitted, I left the college to work in a private consulting capacity. Consequently, I lost contact with Rose.

The years passed and I almost forgot about her. However, I was invited to return to that same college to deliver the commencement address for the graduating class of 1980. As I watched the parade of graduates proudly march across the stage at the Rajah Temple in Reading, Pennsylvania, a little girl appeared, wheeling herself across the ceremonial stage. Yes, it was Rose. She knew she could earn her college degree, and she did it. With no high school diploma, no ability to write, deficient in the ability to speak, incapable of walking—all of those disabilities were not powerful enough to keep that "something inside," Rose's positive self-image, from achieving success. As I looked out into the thousands of mostly unknown faces, I saw them unite to stand to show their appreciation to Rose for the gift that she had given to them—a conviction that if you want some-thing in life, you go for it.

The importance of Rose's success story is magnified by the second experience I had in the same city. Following a motivation workshop that I had conducted with the agents of a real estate firm, one of the salespeople came over to speak with me. The man, who appeared to be in his early thirties, extended his hand to me and initiated the following dialogue:

"Dr. Losoncy," he inquired, "do you remember me?"

Apologetically, I responded, "No, I'm sorry."

"I'm Charles_____, I met you about four or five years ago when you were the Director of Admissions at the community college."

"Were you a student there, Charles?"

"No, but at the time I was thinking about attending the college and studying business."

"And you eventually decided not to go?"

"Yeah. You see, more and more I realized that it would probably be too tough. I mean, uh, at the time I had been out of school for about four or five years and had forgotten almost everything I learned in high school. So I decided against going to school at the time. But maybe someday I'll spend some time reading my old high school books and go to college. But I know that if I went now and competed against those kids fresh out of high school, they would snow me."

Rose, the young woman with cerebral palsy, who lacked an ability to read, write and speak (but had a lot of inner security), now helps people with cerebral palsy. She also inspired a company called Matrix to become a leader in producing professional beauty products.

And Charles, the high school graduate who lacked inner security, is unemployed and still looking for belief in himself. Rose had a disability; she did not have a handicap. Charles did not have a physical disability, but he did have a handicap. He lacked inner security. Who was better off?

The key ingredient for success, the thing inside, was Rose's life inlook, her inner security. The reason Charles failed was not a lack of intelligence, not limited education, nor bad luck, but rather a lack of inner security.

BUILDING YOUR POSITIVE SELF-IMAGE
DEVELOPS YOUR PRACTICAL INTELLIGENCE
(Because a positive self-image works better)

You can change—now. You can make your move toward success at this very moment. You can reach for your dreams by developing yourself, by becoming less dependent upon the outside world, and by starting to use your other potential that has previously been hidden. Give up hidden blaming. You build your inner self by building your own positive self-image.

When your self-image changes, you change your life. Researchers have shown that students have gone from "F" grades to "A" grades in a matter of weeks, salespeople have literally doubled their income; shy people have become respected leaders; depressed people have developed a renewed enthusiasm for life. All of these changes have occurred because of a change in self-image.

Self-image is the ultimate determiner of personal success or failure. Your self-image is so important that one study after another concludes that your view of yourself is the key factor regulating your life. And the great news is that your self-image can change.

In my search for the answer to the question, "Why do people fail?" I chanced upon a writer who could be considered the first advocate of self-image psychology. In his early insightful book, *Self-consistency: A Theory of Personality*, the educator, Prescott Lecky, argued that people fail, more often than not, not because they are incapable of success, but because of their failed self-image. Lecky showed how negative, pre-conceived beliefs and expectations build up resistance and convince people, ahead of time, that it would be impossible for them, with their limited capabilities, to succeed. For example, if a person firmly believes that learning a foreign language would be impossible, the person's self-image will fight, to the bitter end, to keep him or her from achieving success in speaking the new language. The second the foreign language teacher enters the room, the convinced, "determined" person resists the teacher's words.

To disprove the conclusion that this person could not possibly learn the new language, note that people tested and labeled retarded have learned foreign languages. But they only learn when they believe they can. If, however, their self-image resists, they will not learn. And, a more humbling fact, even chimpanzees have learned to understand and respond to the English language. But chimps are lucky. Our hairy friends have an advantage over us. We spend all of our intelligence, reasoning power, and mental energies convincing ourselves that we cannot learn. We conclude that either it would be too difficult to learn or too humiliating to try and maybe fail. If we used just half of that volcano of misdirected failure energy to actively tackle the task instead, we would move toward success. So, fear of failure as a result of a negative self-image is a sure guarantee of failure. With a positive self-image, however, a person envisions success and proceeds ahead to achieve their success.

EXPAND YOUR SELF-IMAGE, EXPAND YOUR PRACTICAL INTELLIGENCE, EXPAND YOUR POSSIBILITIES

Think about your own self-image. Have you ever limited your social possibilities because you believed that there were certain men or women who were out of your social class? If you held these beliefs, what behaviors would your failure beliefs dictate? You probably did not even approach these people to help get the relationship off the ground. Or, if you did approach them, perhaps you said some self-defeating things that sabotaged your chances of developing the relationship. Your self-image actually limited your pool of romantic possibilities. Imagine the number of romantic possibilities you would have by just expanding your self-image!

Did your self-image tell you that you deserve to live in a certain kind of house or that you deserve to have a certain level of income? Did you listen to your self-image and buy that house or work to that exact level of income? And nothing more?

Evidence of the power of self-image is seen everywhere. For example, in the field of organizational development, a common explanation used for decades to demonstrate why promoted people sometimes fail is the well-known Peter Principle, theorized by Dr. Lawrence Peter. People who are competent at one level are sometimes promoted to a higher level. The Peter Principle suggests that because the new level demands different skills, people often fail due to a lack of these new skills. The reason they fail, according to the Peter Principle, is because they were promoted to their level of incompetence.

I believe the Peter Principle is only partially correct. I found another reason to explain why some promoted people fail. If someone is promoted to a new position, but his or her self-image views the position as too difficult or overwhelming, this person will fail. With expanding responsibilities, must come expanded self-image. So, people who are promoted, especially those who are promoted quickly, frequently need self-image expansion. Any organization wishing to tap the fuller potential of its people needs to provide some sort of self-image expansion for its family members.

The owner of a major beauty salon in Florida wanted to raise his prices for haircuts, but the hair stylists working for him resisted the price increases. His employees feared that a price raise would result in a loss of customers. I consulted with the owner, advising him that his hair stylists' resistance was not due to their fear of losing customers, but rather their resistance was a result of their low self-image. They saw their styling abilities at too low a level. Their comment that they would lose customers was simply a comment on their self-image. They believed that they were not worth the new service charge. I advised the enthusiastic owner to help the hair stylists to improve their self-images. This would help them to see their worth in new ways. I asked, "Have you asked them how much they would pay, not for a haircut, but for courage and confidence and hope? Have you helped them to see their profession, not their jobs, in a new light? If you do, and you help your hair stylists to achieve a more positive and expanded self-image, they will beg for the price increase. The price increase is your comment of respect for them. It shows that you believe in them."

As a former college professor, I often heard students make dogmatic comments such as, "I'm a B student" or "I'm an average student." I would always think it funny when one of those B students would get an A and share it almost apologetically with me. When I proudly glanced at the student's A grade, I would enthusiastically respond with "Great job!" Strangely enough, with a self-image lower than the grade the student received, I'd hear something like, "Well, the only reason I received an A was because the professor was easy. I should have earned a B, because I am a B student."

Incredible, isn't it? Have you ever done the samething? Why did the student need to apologize for an A?

WHY DO PEOPLE INITIALLY REJECT NEW POSITIVE IDEAS ABOUT THEMSELVES?

Prescott Lecky explained why the self-image almost always initially rejects a new view of itself. Lecky wrote, "The center or nucleus of the mind is the individual's idea or conception of himself. If a new idea seems consistent with the ideas already present in the system, and particularly with the individual's conception of himself, it is accepted and assimilated easily. If it seems to be inconsistent, it meets with resistance and is likely to be rejected."

Lecky's theory of self-consistency was further supported by researchers who found that a person's self-image of their abilities was a better predictor of how they would achieve than was their IQ. Imagine that! It is not your abilities, but your beliefs about yourself that hold controlling interest in determining whether you will or will not succeed. Imagine the devastating cost of a negative self-image. In the end, if you believe you are incapable of success, your self-image will work overtime to make sure that success will not happen.

Other researchers concluded from their studies that changes in self-image lead to changes in achievement. Again this is powerful and exciting news. Your success is preceded by the belief that you can succeed. If you wanted a few indicators to predict if a student would or would not quit school, start with the student's self-image.

In fact, the key gauge as to how a person will perform in a position is the person's self-image. On these astounding findings, the father of self-image research, William Purvey, writes in relation to school achievement and self-image:

> "The conclusion seems unavoidable. A student carries with him certain attitudes about himself and his abilities which play the primary role in how well he performs in school."

Lecky, in fact, wondered why educators gave students remedial training when what they really needed was an altered and positive vision that reflected the belief "I can and I will learn."

Did you ever see a person labeled "retarded" by one person in the presence of another person who believed in him or her? This person performed much more successfully in the presence of the "believer." Consider yourself. Did you ever have a supervisor who didn't believe in you? Everything you did was viewed negatively. What happened? You probably began to feel incompetent. Conversely, did you ever have a supervisor who enthusiastically encouraged you to recognize your strengths and contributions? What happened? You performed—remember, it was the same you—probably more productively because of the person's beliefs and expectations!

Keep in mind that what you have just read is not opinion—it is a scientifically researched fact. What you see is what you will be!

Concurring with Adler, Lecky, and others, Maxwell Maltz, the world-renowned plastic surgeon, wrote on this topic of self-image:

> *The self-image is the key to human personality and human behavior. The self-image sets the boundaries of individual accomplishment. It defines what you can and cannot be. Expand the self-image and you expand the area of the possible. The development of an adequately realistic self-image will seem to imbue the individual with new capabilities, new talents, and literally turn failure into success (Maltz, 1960, p. xix).*

It is perhaps no news to you that Maltz's book, ***Psycho-Cybernetics***, is one of the best-selling psychological classics of all time. Literally millions of people have been successfully influenced by this "self-determined psychology." Henry Ford's comment, "Believe you can or believe you can't—either way you'll be correct," is in tune with Maltz's, Lecky's, and Adler's observations.

HOW DOES SELF-IMAGE
PRODUCE SUCCESS OR FAILURE?

"I could never speak in front of a group."

"I'm not built to be a leader."

"I'm the kind of person who has difficulty making decisions."

"Me? I'd never make it in sales. Selling requires something I don't have."

"I'm afraid to try new things and take risks."

"Quit smoking? Not me! I lack self-discipline."

"No, I'd never ask her out. She'd never want anything to do with someone like me."

"I guess I have about average intelligence."

"I'm the kind of person who is shy."

"I just can't resist snacks."

"I'm not good at opening up new sales accounts."

"I can't take any pressure on the job. I get migraines when given too much responsibility."

"I'm a 'C' student."

"I've gone about as far as I can."

Have you ever heard any statements like these? Note a few things that each of these statements have in common.

1. Each statement is an echo of an individual's self-image, e.g., "I'm the kind of person who is shy" is a comment on the way the person views him or herself.

2. Each self-image statement is inaccurate, i.e., it can be disproved. As you glance over the list, look closely at each comment and you will see that each conclusion could be challenged.

3. Although each self-image statement is inaccurate, the speaker is not consciously aware that each statement is inaccurate and proceeds through life as if each pronouncement were carved within his or her behavioral granite. The opinion of self is treated by the person as if it were a fact.

4. Each self-image statement limits the individual's potential success. As long as the person believes his or her personal conclusions to be a universal fact, for that exact period of time, no growth can occur. These limits are not very practically intelligent.

5. When the individual's subconscious recognizes that the statement is an inaccurate observation which he or she has treated as if it were a fact, he or she then can attack the false conclusion and proceed to expand the self-defeating self-image to

one of success. This process is called self-image modification and it is the key way of developing practical intelligence.

Would you agree that a positive self-image works better than a negative self-image?

Using your practical intelligence, you become aware of how a person's negative self-image prevents the individual from going forward and invites the individual to get into a blame mode.

Consider the statement, "I could never speak in front of groups."

This comment is a reflection of the speaker's self-image. The speaker acts as if his or her conclusion is an absolute universal fact.

Ask yourself, "What are facts and what are opinions?" Two plus two is a fact. Is "I could never speak in front of groups a fact or an opinion?" Yet the person doesn't know this and treats it as a fact. When the person treats his or her opinion as a fact, this person proceeds based upon the conclusion. These erroneous conclusions direct the person to avoid any situation or opportunity to overcome the "can't." The person's ears quickly perk up to recognize any potentially threatening situation where he or she could possibly be asked to speak and avoids them. So, the person will never experience the chance to disprove the limited conclusion. For the rest of the individual's life, this opinion, treated as fact, will prevent him from achieving success as a public speaker. He needs a change in self-image before success can happen.

"I could never ..." statements are self-defeating. Probably as a toddler the first time you tried to take a step, you fell flat on your face. Suppose you concluded (preverbally, of course) that you could *never* walk like mommy and daddy. If you concluded that, you would never try to walk again. After all, you tried to walk one time and you fell flat or your face so you "could never" walk. Imagine the embarrassment you would experience today arriving at a cocktail party ... crawling! You would scramble into the room and pull the tablecloth down to reach the hors' de oeuvres!

You succeeded because when you fell, your self-image kept envisioning yourself as a person who could or who soon would walk. Fortunately you followed your positive self-image that said you could walk—with practice. You did!

Remember the first time you tried to drive a car? You were probably tense and perhaps your jumpiness caused you to panic and quickly slam on the brakes. Maybe your anxious reaction almost put you and your parents through the front windshield. The earth-shattering experience could have even caused you to break down in tears, proclaiming dogmatically, "I will never learn to do something as tough as driving a car!"

Maybe you even put yourself down even further because you told yourself that the same task of driving appeared to be so easy for everyone else. A negative self-image steered you away from trying again.

Then something happened. At some point your self-image saw hope and "envisioned" success. Your new capable self-image (practical intelligence at work) might have concluded, "It will be tough to drive, but eventually I will learn how." Maybe you had a few more negative experiences while practicing, but each time you improved. You soon succeeded.

Today, with your self-image of "I am capable," you jump into the car, turn on the ignition, turn on the radio, grab your cell phone, dial a number, and one-handedly drive for miles as you glance at the flashing billboards and scenic mountainsides without a single nervous thought, except for your next car payment!

You achieved success simply as a result of a positive self-image that predicted success. Your positive self-image overcame a few failing incidents with a positive hopeful vision. And you wanted to make your actions fit your new vision of yourself as a successful driver.

Now reconsider our friend who proclaims, "I could never speak in front of a group." This person is no different than the young child who could "never walk," or the teenager who could "never drive." This individual is a diamond with a rough, negative self-image, or undeveloped practical intelligence, because this approach isn't working. The culprit denying success for the potential Demosthenes is not a lack of public speaking ability, poor vocabulary, or even fear of groups. The only culprit is the negative self-image that shouts, "I could never." Think of it. Imagine that this person's self-image instead concluded, "It will be tough, but with some work I could speak in front of groups." What a monumental move toward success for the person. Now the blossoming person will develop a new plan of action to overcome these limited visions. A capable and positive self-image is the key ingredient to start the success snowball rolling.

OVERCOMING SELF-IMAGE PROBLEMS: BEEN THERE, DONE THAT!

I chose the example of public speaking because it touches home with me. I would like to share with you a personal story.

A few decades ago, I went to hear a lecture. While watching the dynamic speaker, I became inspired. What he was doing was what I was going to do someday. I became determined to be the best speaker I could be in my lifetime. However, I wasn't talented in speaking. In fact, my vocabulary and grammar scores would win almost any limbo contest. I was frightened to death about even the thought of speaking in front of crowds of people. So I had a lot, a whole lot to overcome.

However, the only resistance I had to overcome was in my mind. I visualized success and I wanted it. I knew there was absolutely no way I wouldn't reach my goal. After all, I had a lifetime.

Because I visualized my goal and became determined, my course was locked in. My compass was pointed toward a goal. My self-image believed that, "With a lot of work, it could be accomplished." So I developed my plan. My ears and eyes were wide open to sense opportunities to observe good speakers. I traveled great distances just to watch speakers' professional mannerisms, demeanor, expressions, words, topic titles. Keep in mind that I would never have done this if my self-image had concluded, ahead of time, that my goal was unattainable.

I started my first lectures by talking with chairs in my living room, imagining that these chairs were real people. Fortunately, there were very few questions following these speeches. I looked into a mirror when I spoke and developed expressive looks and hand gestures. I followed this by taking every opportunity I had to speak to small groups. I worked to improve my vocabulary and grammar. I literally did everything consistent with meeting my goal.

I had many, many setbacks, and still do today, three decades later. It's tough watching people yawn, roll their eyeballs, or leave in the middle of a speech. But remembering my goal, I told myself that these experiences were a necessary part of the journey to reach my destination.

As I think about it today, the destination was inevitable because I visualized my goal and concluded that there was no way I couldn't reach it. When discouraged, my self-image kept envisioning a sign on the highway of life which read:

Next Exit — Nowhere
Straight Ahead — Everywhere

I'm still on that road following my compass that points to success. Today, I make my living through speaking. That tells me that every single time I told myself, "You can never speak in public," I was wrong. I always could. I just needed a self-image that concluded, ahead of time, that the day would come when I would reach my goal. Once I prophesied success, I developed my plan and moved toward my goal. If I made a mistake, I simply corrected the problem. The next time I moved closer to my goal.

On this highway of life, successful achievement of your goals is like driving your car from New York to Los Angeles. When you start, you are at the farthest point from your goal. You cannot possibly be at your goal the moment you start, but you keep focusing on the fact that you are moving toward your goal. Your practical intelligence reminds you that you are getting closer and closer. That view works. If you keep your goal firmly in mind, when your car breaks down, you simply fix it and get on your way. Complaining about the disabled car only wastes your valuable success time and delays your victory celebration.

SELF-IMAGE PROPHESIES
SUCCESS OR FAILURE

David's job interview is only a few minutes away. As the 20 year-old waited tensely outside the personnel manager's office, he thought about how unsuccessful he had been in previous interviews. Reflecting on the last four jobs he didn't get, he thought, "Why should this one be any different?' In addition to being on a job-seeking losing streak, he reminded himself about all of the news on how tight the job market was. In addition he was certain that there are many, many people much more qualified for this job than he is. Although his background fits the requirements on paper, he is sure there will be someone else who has either more experience, more education, or more of an "in." He slumped in his chair as he looked around the room. It is crowded with competition, he is sure, for the same job. And he is sure that everyone of them has something that he lacks. To escape eye-to-eye contact with his competitors, he glanced at the secretary. She appears to be meticulously organized and aloof. She peered at David over the top of her glasses and gave him an intimidating look. David squirmed again. His heart is pounding, his voice seems to be leaving him, his palms are sweating, his chin is quivering, and his knees are shaking. He wants to leave, but at that moment, the personnel manager opened the door and announced his name, requesting that he come into the office.

Jonathan is also waiting for a job interview. It's only a few minutes away. This 20 year-old man is waiting outside the personnel manager's office with eager anticipation. He begins to think about how he can be a success on the job once he gets the position. He analyzes the position he is seeking and lives a day in the life of a person in that capacity. It is a position in which he would be dealing with people. Jonathan then imagines that he owns the company. He wonders what kind of a person he would want in that position for his company. What kind of attitudes would he be looking for in people he would hire? He concludes that he would want a person who likes people, is confident, is open for new ideas, is enthusiastic, and who would make a good company employee. Yes, Jonathan thinks, to be a good company employee, it would be wise to learn even more about the company. He looks around the reception area and finds a company brochure on the table. He pages through the brochure and becomes increasingly excited about the company. He learns some interesting facts about the size and scope of the operation. This news excites him and tells him of the opportunities to grow. Jonathan looks at the many offices and imagines himself with an office of his own someday soon. The secretary, obviously efficient, stares over her glasses at him, and Jonathan gives her a big ear-to-ear smile. She smiles back. Jonathan feels great and thinks how warm the people are here at this company. He is also impressed with her efficiency and kindly shares his observation with her.

Impressed, he comments, "I really admire your organization. Are you one of those naturally organized people?" The secretary replies, "I guess I enjoy my work." She smiles again. He already feels he belongs there. And he does. And he soon will be.

The door opened and the personnel manager invited Jonathan into his office.

David and Jonathan are stories of life. David's negative self-image dictated to his whole viscera the notion that he did not deserve the position and that he would never get it. As a result, David's self-image vigorously worked to defeat him. The personnel manager, reading David's confidence level, saw him as a person who would be too timid, too defensive, to be part of a growing, assertive company. David did not get the position and he was defeated again. For the next job interview, his self-image will be even more negative. The young man's self-image predicted failure and the prediction was accurate. Low practical intelligence develops a view of life that doesn't work.

Jonathan, on the other hand, carries a self-image that announces the arrival of success. Jonathan predicted success for himself and thus used his energies to make that success happen. While David squirmed in his seat, Jonathan learned more about the company, imagining what kind of employee the company needed in that position, and, in fact, ignited his own enthusiasm for the job.

David and Jonathan faced the same situation. David and Jonathan's college grades were the same. Yet observe how different the situation looked to each because of different self-images. David saw obstacles. Jonathan saw opportunities.

If you were the personnel manager, who would you hire?

Your self-image produces success or failure by prophesizing or subconsciously predicting success or failure before it happens. And self-image, more often than not, is accurate. Practical intelligence tells us that moving ahead with certainty gives you the winner's edge.

In this chapter we have further developed our practical intelligence by becoming intrinsically motivated, driven from within. With our security inside of us, we no longer need to lean on the world for reinforcement and support. It is inside us.

Now, let's improve our practical intelligence by finding ways of humorously accepting and loving tough realities in the world.

> *"If it weren't for all the things that shouldn't be (according to me), I could be happy!"*

5

ACCEPTANCE

Frees Us Faster Than Blaming Reality

LOVE WHAT YOU CAN'T CHANGE. WHY? BECAUSE YOU DON'T HAVE TO DWELL ON IT ANYMORE

I love the weather. I was going to be a meteorologist until I found out math was involved. And, on top of that, science. All of us "discipline problems" were pretty good at math because whenever we acted up in grade school, the nun would give us math drill cards to do after school. And it seemed to me that after doing the late weather at 11 p.m., I wouldn't want to hang around dividing seven digit numbers by four digit numbers.

Anyway, I love the weather, and my favorite station is the weather channel. Why? Because it is a place where I can relax. I don't have the same tension that I have when I watch Regis ask questions and then don't get them right or run out of lifelines. I do not play a role in the weather. I can watch it unfold. Unlike a TV program or a movie, when people are just getting paid to say the words of a writer, the weather is real. I love the weather because the pressure is off me.

I can't change the weather. I love things I can't change. I can take my energies somewhere else. That's where the pressure is on.

REALITY HAS MORE IMPORTANT THINGS TO DO THAN TO PUT CHALLENGES IN MY WAY

When the light turns red, it means stop. Nothing more, nothing less. Some people give that light more power than it has. Perhaps you have even seen people talk to traffic lights, even yell at them. I suspect that the light is unaffected by this useless monologue.

But some of my friends who are unbendingly determined to make themselves miserable at every opportunity, caution me that if you yell at the light long enough, and loud enough, it will soon change. They are right. The light will change in about 30–45 seconds either way!

When we find ourself on what seems to be a bumpy road and realize that it is actually a flat tire, the person with practical intelligence decides that a great choice would be to pull over and fix the flat tire. Nothing more, nothing less. The person who is a little slower to grasp what is happening here, immediately goes into the blame mode, mentally searching for people and things to blame.

"These tires are no good."

"This car always has a problem."

"If my boss had given me that pay raise I deserve, I could have bought better tires."

"These roads are rotten."

"My wife forgot to send in my AAA renewal card. I'll have to pay to have this thing towed."

"Why didn't I put a spare in the car after the last flat?"

This type of blaming, of course, could go on forever. The number of things we blame for our situation is only limited to our creative mind's determination to avoid taking action and solving the problem. Remember, these events are neither good nor bad. They just are!

The person with practical intelligence wants to make the connection between cause and effect and then solve the problem.

"Hmm, the car is wobbling, but the road looks fine. It must be a flat tire. Thank God, I realized what the problem was. I'll pull over to the side and check on it. I'll probably have the car towed since I don't have a spare."

Notice: stress free by solving instead of blaming.

Love the things you can't change. Why? Because you don't have to worry about them. You can't change them anyway. And then focus your energies on the things you can change.

I FOUGHT REALITY AND REALITY WON

I believe that life is incredibly simple and that it is people who make it complex. Most people frustrate themselves and make their lives difficult by making everything THE ULTIMATE HUMAN EXPERIENCE—the mistake of losing sight of reality: 99% of us are partially out of touch with reality at one time or another. These are the times when we confuse "what we wish to be" with "what actually is" in life. We reduce ourselves to having the intelligence of a dog chasing the wheels of a car. Instead, succeed by saving your-self a lot of energy by chiseling these three words into your mental fabric: "What Is, Is."

Motivational lectures and positive attitude books often neglect an important point about reality. Your start toward Success City is reality. If you are so high that you think you could fly, it would be a grave error to ignore the reality of the law of gravity. As Bertrand Russell once commented, "Any man who maintains that happiness comes wholly from within should be prepared to spend thirty-six hours in rags in a blizzard without food." This point is not meant to discourage you. I feel, perhaps, a parental need to not have you fall flat on your face. That will only discourage you and keep you from being successful, thus not helping the rest of humanity. We need you. So face the fact that there will be barriers, but through creative thinking, enthusiasm, and goal setting, these obstacles can be overcome. So when I say, "What Is, Is," it is meant to encourage you. When you accept this fact of reality, you have an invigorating, challenging starting point. Dreamers who faced reality and learned how to reach the heavens despite the realities of gravity were those who designed planes and spacecraft. Wishers, on the other hand, who didn't take reality into consideration only experienced frustration. Increase your practical intelligence by getting a keen sense of reality. Never again be frustrated by putting reality "where it isn't."

SEEING REALITY FOR WHAT IT IS

Lock your mind forever on these three facts about reality, and you will find yourself managing your life by a realistic goal orientation:

FACT 1: Reality is not what we wish it to be; rather, reality is what it is.

FACT 2: Reality is not interested in what each of us thinks it "should be:" rather, reality is what it is.

FACT 3: Reality is not just or fair; rather, reality is what it is.

FACT

1

Reality is not what we wish it to be; rather, reality is what it is.

Don't get caught in the "wisher's web." Reality has no respect for wishers. Wishing away a thunderstorm or wishing a million-dollar-lottery win are almost guaranteed routes to failures. Not only is wishing an ineffective course of action, but it is a frustrating route as well. That is what concerns me about you. I don't want you to be discouraged in your trip to Success City because you made the error of wishing that the 200-mile journey was only 50 miles and eventually became frustrated. It is 200 miles. But after facing reality head on, if you use creative thinking and enthusiasm, you will find a way. People living in the Sea of Fantasy off of the Coast of Reality dream up a world that doesn't exist, and then they get frustrated when the world they wished for "lets them down." The world, in fact, didn't let them down. The problem was that they were living on wishes which were a false "pick-me-up" in the first place. If you want to eat, stop wishing and start fishing. Don't compromise one moment of your dream; just make sure that you are clear that your starting point is on firm ground.

FACT

2

Reality is not interested in what each of us thinks it "should be;" rather, reality is what it is.

Most of the people in the world beat their heads against the wall of reality by confusing what they think "should be" with what actually is. If you take the following sentence and make it a part of your life, you will never again be unhappy or frustrated for more than just a few seconds. Here it is: THERE ARE NO SHOULDS, OUGHTS, OR MUSTS IN THE WHOLE WORLD ... NONE! EVERY TIME WE SAY ANY OF THOSE WORDS, WE ARE RUNNING FULL FORCE AWAY FROM REALITY. INSTEAD OF SAYING "SHOULD," "OUGHT," OR "MUST," LEARN THE ONLY WORDS THAT WILL LEAD TO SUCCESS. What are those magic words? They are WHAT IS MY PLAN? Observe how people sit in their SHOULD seats and run away from reality. Allow me to share a few of my experiences with SHOULD thinkers.

A client of mine who came late for one of our appointments told me apologetically, "I'm sorry I'm late, but I caught ten red lights in a row. No one should never get that many." My response was the only logical one I could give. I asked Barb, "Exactly how many red lights SHOULD you get? Think about it.

While speaking at a teachers' convention in Edmonton, Alberta, one of the bellhops at the hotel apologized to me for the freezing weather. "I responded again in the only logical way I knew. I asked, "How cold SHOULD it be?" He had, believe it or not, an answer. He knocked my socks off by responding, "It should be about ten degrees warmer." I wasn't finished with his comment that "it SHOULD be about ten degrees warmer." I asked, "WHATS YOUR PLAN?"

A fellow professor with whom I once shared an office was angrily hovering over his desk one day saying, "I left my car keys on the desk. They SHOULD be there! Looking at the empty desk, I retorted, "But they're not." While pointing accusingly to his desk, he came back with, "But they SHOULD be." "But they're not," I said again. "But they SHOULD be," he growled. Then I said, "It seems to me that the keys, whether they SHOULD or SHOULD **NOT** be on your desk, are, in fact, not on your desk. Believe me, there is a greater chance that your keys are in Rio than there is of them being here on your desk. So there are at least two things you could do. You could, for the rest of your life, stand by this desk and say, "The keys SHOULD be here" or you could look elsewhere. Which decision would help you to find your keys?

Another friend of mine, who usually was quite in touch with reality, had a weak moment. Quite annoyed, Carol said to me, "My oil burner broke down and it SHOULD not have. It was just checked, and I even have a warranty."

I asked, "Did you show the oil burner the warranty?" I went on to add, "For the rest of your life, you can stand by the oil burner, chanting, 'You SHOULD work, you SHOULD work, because I have a warranty,' or you call to get it fixed. Take just a few minutes to think the matter through."

Which would be a more productive course of action?

Finally, I can't leave this topic on reality until I relate an incredible experience. At a party, I listened to someone say that she had just started a diet. I was elated about her goal-setting spirit. Soon the hostess came around with a tray, serving cake and ice cream. When the bright-eyed hostess turned to us, she enticed my friend, who had just claimed she started a diet that day, by asking, "Would you care for some marble cake and ice cream?"

Hold on to your sombrero when you hear, in this chapter on reality, my friend's response.

"Oh, I SHOULDN'T have any cake ... but I guess it won't hurt!

I looked at her and responded, "What would be your second guess?"

Yes, LIFE IS INCREDIBLY SIMPLE, but people make it difficult when they do as psychologist Albert Ellis says: "They SHOULD on themselves."

Eliminate the words "should, "ought," and "must" and instead say, "WHAT IS MY PLAN?" You will be amazed how many people who fail have vocabularies filled with those productive words. Become a "WHAT'S-MY-PLAN?" thinker.

FACT

3

Reality is not just or fair; rather, reality is what it is.

It would do my heart and mind a lot of good if I didn't have to write this because it is inconsistent with my former strongly held beliefs. But it appears to me that if you want to succeed and help the world, you need to accept the fact that REALITY IS NEITHER JUST NOR FAIR. The minute that we allow this insight to permeate our minds, that's the minute that we can bring about a positive change. Observe Kathy, who's caught in the unfairness trap:

> Kathy: It just isn't fair. Carolyn can eat all the pastry she wants and she never gains a pound. Yet, if I so much as look at cakes or cookies, I put on weight.

Where can Kathy take her complaint? Right, there is nowhere to go! Kathy is producing her own frustration because she believes that reality is not fair to her. Her frustration, remember, is not due to the fact she gains weight, but is related to her unwillingness to accept reality the way it "is." Imagine if Kathy accepted the fact that she gains weight easily and used all of her energies to plan her diet, instead of using her energies to complain. Kathy is destined to a life of frustration because she does not accept an element of the world that she believes does not work in her favor.

We might say to Kathy, "Yes, it is unfair. But maybe, if you think about it, the unfairness of life has actually worked pretty well in your favor. For example, you have a healthy heart, you eat three meals a day, you have the ability to read, and you have two TV's. Most of the people in the world would enthusiastically change places with you at this moment. Yes, it's true, the world is unfair, but look at what you have and develop a plan to help other people."

It is important for me to say here that justice is a most noteworthy ideal and that I would be glad to be right up front leading the parade for a more just world. But it's a fact that the world is not just or fair, and demanding that it be so is not only ineffective, but it is frustrating. Together, let's develop a plan to change that fact.

JUST BECAUSE YOU CAN'T DO EVERYTHING DOESN'T MEAN YOU CAN'T DO ANYTHING

Once the person who has developed his practical intelligence meets reality head-on, face to face, and decides that he would rather accept what he chooses to not change rather than to fight an uphill battle, his energies are freed to face the challenges on level ground.

I can't live forever. I can't fly without help. But I can:

1. choose my attitude

2. compliment a friend

3. smile

4. exercise and feel great afterward

5. dress up

6. choose what I will eat tonight

7. write a poem

8. decide between a Mounds Bar and an Almond Joy the next time I am in a store

9. think of people who love me

10. go to the public library

11. say "I'm sorry"

12. give a hug

13. make a child's day

14. create

15. listen

16. sing

17. write a poem

18. forgive

19. take a walk

20. take a hot bath

21. jump rope

22. climb a tree

23. listen to favorite music

24. have dinner tonight with candle light

25. buy someone a card

26. make a card for someone

27. try to make my own soft pretzels

28. go to a movie

29. thank someone for doing something very ordinary

30. see the people around me in new, fresh, exciting ways

31. leave a note at home for my loved ones to discover

32. remember how much I wanted my spouse a few years back

33. go to a public park

34. bounce a ball

35. include somebody who feels left out

36. set new goals

37. borrow a dog

38. read a positive book

39. write a letter to the President and see if I get one back

40. try to do a pushup

41. enroll in a karate class and see if I can get to the second belt

42. realize how great a really good apple or pear can taste

43. imagine anything

44. mix ice cream flavors together to create a new one

45. try to guess how fast elephants can run

46. conduct a survey with people on a topic I am interested in

47. read the **Guinness Book of Records** and see which one I have the best chance of beating

48. take the Coke or Pepsi test and see how accurate I am

49. go to a flower shop

50. estimate the number of steps it takes me to walk the block in front on my house

Just because you can't live forever or fly by yourself today doesn't mean you can't do anything.

WHEN SOMEONE SAYS, "FACE REALITY," THANK THEM!

A friend of mine was listening to one of my wild ideas and stopped me with a "face reality." He was focusing in on all of the barriers I would face in attempting to get this idea off the ground. At first, his comment stopped my momentum. I started reflecting on the challenges, the problems, and the probabilities and found myself creating my own discouragement. I was subconsciously blaming reality. It shouldn't be this difficult.

Then I thought about his words, "face reality," in a different way. If I am going to face reality, the starting point of reality is that "I am alive. And that wouldn't have to be!"

So I turned to my friend who had just cautioned me to face reality and shook his hand, before I ran up the street inspired.

But first, I exclaimed, "Thank you so much, Bob. Occasionally I do forget to face reality. Occasionally I do forget that I am alive, and lucky enough to have a great wife and daughter, to have a good job, to live in America, and to be in good health, eat three meals a day, and have a home, and a car. Thank you.

Sometimes we hear "face reality" the wrong way—the way that doesn't work. Develop your practical intelligence and face reality. And thank others when they remind you to do so as well.

YOU ARE TRYING WAY TOO HARD

After arriving in Dallas to speak at a convention, a man stopped me in the hallway and said, "I didn't know you were going to be at the convention. I am so excited to meet you. I am going to try to get into your talk tomorrow morning."

I grabbed my heart, looking all fatigued, weak, and drained, and responded, "Oh no, please, please don't try. I'm already burned out just thinking about how hard you are going to have to work at trying. In fact, you now have to do two things to get to the talk. First, you have to try. Then, second, you are going to have to get there. This is over-whelming, my heart is beating fast, I'm sweating, I'm close to having an anxiety attack. Everytime I have to try, it usu-ally is so overwhelming and draining, that I can't get it done."

I stopped for a moment to observe his confused face and added, "My friend, don't make it so hard on yourself. Stop trying and instead just show up in the Enterprise Room at 8 a.m. But if you have to try, you'll never make it."

When I arrived at 7 a.m. the next morning, there was my newfound friend already seated, the first one in the classroom.

"I see you didn't try to get here today, huh?" I asked.

"No way. This was too important for me to try to be here. I just decided to be here. It was effortless," he responded.

When you ask your daughter to clean up her room, and she tells you she'll try, let her know that you are not asking that much of her.

"Oh honey, I'm not asking you to go that far. I'm not asking you to do two things, first to try and then to actually do. I'm just asking that you take action and clean up your room. It'll be so much easier if you don't have to try first."

After a confused silence, you'll start to hear the vacuum cleaner. You've taken away the hard work of trying so that she can effortlessly go about the business of cleaning up her room.

WATCH YOUR LANGUAGE

We don't know reality directly; we know it through the words we choose to use. Words are powerful, emotional triggers.

In *What is, is!*, Diane Losoncy and I suggested words to eliminate from our vocabulary to develop our practical intelligence.

Eliminate, "shoulds," "oughts," and "musts." We learned these from our teacher, Albert Ellis. As I discussed earlier in this chapter, reality is not the way we want it to be; reality is the way it is. Some people get angry and blame the world for it not being the way they want it to be. They then demand that the universe adjust itself to be more convenient for them. You can see their demands in the frequent uses of the words "should," "ought," and "must."

Consider the grandiosity inherent in these statements:

"The weather shouldn't be this cold in June."

"I went to Europe to visit. I was only there a few days and came home. There are too many foreigners there. There oughta be more Americans."

"My car must not run out of gas just because it's on empty."

Curiously there is not a single should, ought or must in the real world. We create our own ideal (ideal for me) world every time we use one of these words. Plus, we run away from the real world of "What is, is!" We produce our own frustration when we demand that the world should be better for us than it is.

As we eliminate the shoulds, oughts, and musts, let's find more rational words to take the sting out of our psychic pain.

Language Problem	Language Revealing Practical Intelligence
"It shouldn't be this cold."	"I would prefer that it was warmer, but it is 2 degrees. I'll bundle up."
"There oughta be more Americans."	"I personally would feel more comfortable if there were more Americans in Europe, but what is, is."
"My car must not run out of gas."	"It would be more convenient for me if my car made it to a gas station, but when there is no more gas in the car, then it is what is called, 'out of gas.' It needs gas and will stop without it. This not a personal event because anybody whose car is out of gas would also have a car that would stop."

DEVASTATED OR INCONVENIENCED?

Since events become whatever we label them, we play a role in how much an event impacts us by the words we choose to give to the event.

While speaking about turning catastrophes into inconveniences to a group of about 1500 hair stylists in Des Moines, Iowa, I tripped over my microphone wire. I fell off the stage and landed on the floor. The group of midwesterners were polite and concerned. As I picked myself up and walked back onto the stage, I said, "That, for example, was an inconvenience."

The silence was broken as the group started to chuckle.

"Yes," I ad-libbed, "that was an inconvenience. Why? Because I fell and I hurt myself a little. Was it a tragedy? No. Could it have been? Yes, of course, if I had called it a 'tragedy.' If I had labeled the event a 'tragedy,' I probably would not have walked back onto the stage. I also might have stopped speaking for a living. Or I could have made it a catastrophe by calling it a catastrophe. But I choose to call it an inconvenience. So that is what it becomes to me."

I continued, "Now, to be honest with you, did I want to fall? Well, if it was on a ballot, I would have voted, 'no.' But should I have fallen? Of course, because the only thing underneath my feet was air. I had to fall!"

Years later, a woman in that group moved to Wyoming. One evening, she drove her car into the front of her salon. Her husband was in the car with her. Can you imagine? There she was in her car, in her salon, in a state of panic. And all of a sudden, remembering the program in Iowa, she started to laugh and cry at the same time. She turned to her husband and said, "This is just an inconvenience." They backed their car out, hugged, and planned their new salon.

Years later she told me, "Dr. Lew, you have to come see our new salon. It's beautiful. And, you know, fortunately, we've only been through a minor inconvenience. Had we been through a tragedy, we could never have bounced back. But to only go through a minor inconvenience, like we did, it doesn't take long to rebuild."

Watch your language. Don't make a tough reality tougher. You get tougher and the tough reality melts in your will.

THANK YOUR CRITICS
FOR THE FREE ADVICE

Part of dealing with reality is handling criticism from others. The person who needs practical intelligence development, when criticized:

- gets hurt

- attacks the critic ("You're not so hot yourself")

- defends ("If it weren't for ...")

- denies

- most unfortunately, misses information

On the other hand, the person with high practical intelligence welcomes criticism as a source of potential learning. When criticized, he listens to the criticism and simply asks himself the question, "How can I use the information he is giving me to help me become a better person?"

You'll notice, there is no pain, hurt, anger, or desire for revenge and no defensiveness—just a simple determination to learn and to grow.

Think of the last time someone criticized you. Block out everything but the person's words and your desire to focus in on how you can use the person's words to become the best you can be. Let it in.

Make a mental note of what you learned.

Now respond defensively and personally to the critic's attack and see what you learn and how you feel.

You probably sense that when you handled the criticism with practical intelligence and a desire to learn and grow, you didn't get upset or hurt, didn't experience anger or a desire for revenge, didn't think of the critic's imperfections, and, most importantly, you got information that can help you to grow.

Maybe you even had a desire to thank the critic. All of those benefits came to you by making a choice to accept reality instead of blaming it. That's why that decision is called practical intelligence—because it works much, much better.

Instead of blaming reality, we develop our practical intelligence to not only accept, but to love things we choose not to change. Now let's find ways of encouraging people in our home or workplace rather than blaming them.

> *"If it weren't for other people,
> I could succeed"*

6

ENCOURAGING OTHERS

*Gets Better Results
Than Blaming Them*

A PERSONAL EXPERIENCE
ON THE POWER OF ENCOURAGEMENT

I graduated 309 out of 321 at Reading Central Catholic High school in Pennsylvania. This actually appears better than it really was because I had some teachers who gave me the benefit of the doubt, at the last minute, finding a way to turn that F into the D. Even today, I keep telling myself that their motivations were not to have me repeat their class the following year.

In my junior year, at one point I was failing five out my six subjects, which the cigar-smoking principal asked me to justify.

"How do you explain this, Lewis? Five F's and a D!"

"I'm just putting too much time in on that subject I'm getting a D in," I analyzed."

Fr. Leichner didn't seem to understand.

The same year, an English teacher suggested that I might have been copying from another student.

"Lewis, you had ninety-nine correct out of a hundred."

"Thank you, Sister."

"Lewis, I noticed that you sat right beside David. And David is our top student."

"I don't remember where I sat that day."

"Well, interestingly, David, our top student, also like you, Lewis, had ninety-nine right out of a hundred."

"Wow, I'm in good company, Sister."

"And even more interesting Lewis, is that both you and David missed the same question, number 56."

"He and I must think alike, Sister."

"Or is it possible that you were copying from David, Lewis?"

I sensed where she was going with this. And I knew I could help her with her concerns. I had this bright idea.

"Sister, how about if we look at both papers, David's and mine. If we both wrote the same answer for number 56, the one we both had wrong, that would certainly prove one of us had copied. But, if we had two different answers for number 56, then that is proof that neither David nor I were copying. Do you agree? Doesn't that make sense?"

"I guess it does," she hesitatingly responded.

She got both papers out, and I proved to her that I could not have been copying because, fortunately for both of us, we had two different answers for number 56. I'll never forget it.

David wrote, "I don't know."

And I wrote, "Neither do I."

It was there, that day, that I found out that two people looking at the same thing could see two different things in it.

But, back to the encouragement. One day, while walking down the school halls, our guidance counselor, who was also a priest, stopped me, looked me in the eyes, and smiled.

"You are fantastic!"

I never recalled a dialogue like this before. I wondered what his angle was.

"Could you tell me just a little bit more, Father?"

"Yes, I saw two nuns walking down the hallways, and you had them so upset I think the one was almost swearing."

"Is that good?"

"Well, it sure shows you have a talent."

"What's that?"

"Well if you can make nuns swear, it shows that you have the ability to influence people. Did you ever think about how you could use that talent?"

"I never knew I had it, until now."

"Well someday, you could become a teacher or a salesman."

Somebody saw something positive in me. That night I went home and I did something rare. I studied. And the next day I got a B+ on a geometry test. Who did I take my grade to? Of course, my encourager. And the good priest looked me in the eyes again, and suggested that I could focus on my weaknesses or I could focus on my strengths. He asked me which approach I thought would work better.

My encourager changed my life by helping me see what was right with me. I was so accustomed to hearing about my deficiencies and what was wrong that I thought my weaknesses defined me. I learned that a person has both positives and negatives and that successful people choose to focus on the positives.

Like the positive priest, we can choose to see what is right with people. I believe that the priest, and our own experiences, would tell us this approach works better than blaming people and centering on their weaknesses.

In the workplace, we can blame people for being lazy or we can develop approaches to encourage them.

ON ENCOURAGEMENT IN THE WORKPLACE, SURVEY SAYS ...

In life, it becomes clear, after a while, that blaming another person for being lazy doesn't exactly motivate them, except to defend, makes excuses, fight back, blame us, etc., etc. And then the vicious cycle gets worse, and we find ourselves way off the issue. In *The Motivating Team Leader*, I listed the qualities that people gave me in a survey as being present in their most discouraging and most encouraging leaders. The responses were so significant because there were so many areas of agreement.

First, related to the qualities of the most discouraging leader:

1. Always pointed out what I was doing wrong, never what I was doing right.

2. Never listened to me.

3. Had double standards, one for his favorites, another for the everyone else.

4. Knew it all.

5. Stole my ideas.

6. Had no time for me.

7. Didn't trust me.

8. Talked down at me.

9. Gave me false hopes.

10. Belittled me.

11. Made me feel like an underdog.

12. Took advantage of me.

13. Gave me only negative feedback.

14. Set up inconsistent rules.

15. Lied.

16. Would fly off the handle. I lived in fear when he was around.

17. Took on all of my responsibilities. I felt like I was totally unimportant.

18. Used her position to overpower me.

19. Gave no direction. I didn't even know what doing a good job meant.

20. Said things like, "I'll see you in my office after work." He said it the first thing in the morning.

21. Intimidated and stressed me.

22. Put my ideas down.

23. Kept giving me extra things to do without ever even saying thanks.

24. Had a negative attitude.

25. Saw me as important only as someone who produced. Never noticed that I was a person.

26. Constantly compared me to other people.

27. Made me feel unwanted. At staff meetings, he never even looked at me.

28. Was a smooth talker, but had no substance.

29. Was never satisfied—was a nit picker.

30. Told how much he produced when he was in the job before me.

31. Always had to get the last word in.

32. Insisted that I take on his responsibilities, such as dealing with tough, angry customers.

33. Yelled at me in front of others. I felt so small.

34. Played favorites.

35. Socialized with men but not the women. It gave men the edge for promotion.

36. Had critical facial expressions. I especially remember the heavy eyebrows.

37. I would beat my brains out working on something and it was never noticed.

38. Used sarcasm and embarrassment.

39. Assumed I knew what he wanted or what he was thinking.

40. Was closed-minded

Now, here is a list of the responses about the most encouraging leader:

1. Listened to me. He really listened.

2. Believed in me, even more than I believed in myself.

3. Noticed what I did right, as well as pointing areas where I could develop myself.

4. Delegated responsibility.

5. Enthusiastic.

6. Has a sense of humor.

7. Admitted he made mistakes.

8. Gave me credit for my ideas.

9. Recognized when I needed a lift and was there.

10. Was interested in me as a person.

11. Was at peace with himself.

12. Was consistent.

13. Was a good teacher, willing to share ideas.

14. Criticized constructively.

15. Followed through on promises.

16. Was honest, genuine, real.

17. Was positive.

18. Permitted freedom and independence as long as I got the job done. I didn't feel smothered or claustrophobic.

19. Gave me a feeling that things I said in confidence would be left in confidence.

20. Said "hello" or "glad to see you" each morning.

21. I heard comments from my manager's boss about me like, "Bob tells me what a great job you are doing." That really gave me a lift.

22. Accepted me even if I pointed out how things could be better in the department or if I criticized him.

23. Showed how what I did for the company was important.

24. Helped me feel like part of the team.

25. Did little things like to reassure me after I came back from vacation that I was missed.

26. I knew exactly what was expected of me.

27. I felt very creative around him. Even if he didn't like my idea, he would still appreciate my efforts.

28. My first day on the job he took me around to meet everybody. I felt immediately accepted.

29. Was fair, but firm.

30. Vulnerable. Share his own shortcomings.

31. Was always available to talk to me. Gave me time.

32. Believed in me. I felt special and unique, and so did everybody.

33. Remembered our conversations.

34. Was open-minded.

35. Was non-defensive.

36. Gave good leadership. Lifted the team's spirits. Saw obstacles as challenges.

37. Was a terrific example. I even quit smoking and started dieting from her example. She was a total person.

38. Professional—never used backbiting or putting people down. Even when attacked, he listened and rationally explained his position.

39. Warm, but not warmth stemming from weakness.

40. After disciplining me, he gave me hope and a new start.

11 ENCOURAGING APPROACHES TO SPARK PEOPLE UP

1 **Make each person you meet feel significant.** Meet people in a special way. In a world where every one is a number at most places they go, quickly recognize the person who is inside the worker, the clerk, the custodian, or whatever it is they do. Treat them like the unique person they are. Genuinely care and spend more than 50% of your conversation time talking about them and their interests and concerns. Use his or her name frequently and make it a point to remember special details.

2 **Focus on strengths and potential.** Condition yourself to focus in on what's right with people rather than dwelling on what's wrong. We all know people who are nit pickers and flaw finders and are experts on seeing what is wrong. Be an individual who is finely tuned to see what's right in the other person.

Develop your strength-focusing skills by conditioning yourself to immediately zero in on the assets and potential in the people you meet.

Be a "pick-em-up" type of person with everyone you meet. You've heard the expression, "Here comes bad news!" Be a good news giver so that when people see you, your very presence gives them a lift.

Develop the talent to see assets even in people's liabilities and weaknesses. Remember what the encouraging guidance counselor did for me: he saw my strengths under my weaknesses.

3 **Be quick to recognize progress and improvement.** Your child is so excited. The three year old puts on her own shoes for the first time. But they're on backward. She can't wait to see the look in your eyes as she sways over to you to feature her proud

achievement. She has seen adults put on shoes before. She has dreamed of the day that she could finally do it. She worked at it. She took a risk. She's ready and comes over to you and says, "Look, I put my own shoes on all by myself!" I hope you don't respond with, "They're on the wrong feet!" Recognize her progress and improvement: "Honey, you put your own shoes on, all by yourself. You must be so proud of yourself. You are growing up, aren't you?"

4 **Communicate your confidence.** Goethe, the poet, concluded that, "If you want someone to develop a trait, treat them as though they already have it." Make a winner out of people. Communicate that you believe in them. They can do it!

Researchers have shown that when teachers have greater positive expectations for students, they actually help to provide a climate where students produce better grades. When bogus psychological reports were given to teachers, telling them that the I.Q. scores of individuals were higher than they actually were, the teachers' elevated expectations of the students' abilities led to greater student achievement. In *Unconscious Conspiracy: Why Leaders Can't Lead*, Warren Bennis stated, "In a study of school teachers, it turned out that when they had high expectations of their students, that alone was enough to cause an increase of up to twenty five points in the student's I.Q. scores."

Robert Schuller, founder of the concept of possibility thinking, told about on an elderly school teacher from New York who had a high rate of success with students whose peers had a high frequency of brushes with the law. When asked for the secret of her success, the teacher said, "I just loved those kids and believed in them."

If someone believes in us, and communicates that belief in us along with understanding and a feeling that what I do is important, I will have a tendency to take a second look at myself. Deep down I want that person to be right, so I might try to make it happen. The fact that some psychologists tell us that we use only 2–15% of our potential demonstrates that there is always room for improvement—in the context of an encouraging person.

What we expect is, more often than not, what we get.

5 **Choose understanding before judging.** Consciously choose to listen to understand another person based upon their vantage point. What does it look like from their world? Not how should it look to the other person according to my world.

A little boy came home from school and said, "Mommy, that mean teacher yelled at me in front of all the other kids." The average parent responds judgmentally asking, "What did you do?"

The child, of course, answers, "Nothing!" and shuts down.

The listening parent imagines what it looked like and felt like from the child's perspective.

"Dillon, that must have been embarrassing. I mean being yelled at in front of your friends."

Dillion now opens up, tears in his eyes. "It was, Mama."

And Mom responds, "Would you like to tell me more about what happened today?"

"Ok, mom."

Notice that "Would you like to tell me more about what happened today?" Is the same question as "What did you do?" except that it works better. Listening to understand is a sure sign of practical intelligence.

6 **Help each person see how he or she fits in.** Alfred Adler argued that humans are socially rooted beings and it is important for a person to see where he or she fits in.

"We really missed you while you were on vacation. We had less fun when our stand-up comedian was away," helps a person see how they fit in, how they belong.

"Without you in the lineup, Bill, we have no power."

"As our receptionist, you're the first lady of our business."

"You are a symbol to our team of the importance of teamwork, Ally."

Think of people you want to encourage and find ways to help them to see how they fit in, what role they play, and how they belong. Their eyes will light up when you do.

7 **Point out each person's contribution to the world.** A day that will stand out in the history books for centuries to come is July 20, 1969. It was a day when humankind's grasp became closer to its reach. It was a day when the citizens of the planet Earth placed the first person on the moon, one quarter million miles away. It was a proud day for all Earthlings, especially Americans.

July 20, 1969 was an especially proud day for me. It was all because of a special meaning-giving leader for whom I worked. Let me explain the power of a meaning-giving leader.

In the summer months from 1963-1967, I was employed by Carpenter Technology, a Reading, Pennsylvania-based specialty steel company. My job was a bundler. We bundled bars of steel over and over for eight hours a day, six days a week. Sound boring? It could have been, but I was fortunate enough to have a far-sighted foreman who helped point out to each of us bundlers what we really were doing for the world.

"Part of what you guys are bundling today will be headed for Detroit and will become part of automobiles," the burly enthusiast might say at the beginning of the shift. But the one meaning-giving day that I remember the most was when Mr. U confided, "This week most of what you fellas will be bundling up to ship out is a specialty product designed to be a part of the first space vehicle, like the one our government will eventually be landing on the moon."

Man, did we bundle that day.

On that July day when American astronaut Neil Armstrong took his first step on the moon and voiced those words, "One small step for a man, one giant leap for mankind," I was nose up to the TV, tears in my eyes, waiting for him to give ... the list of credits!

I dreamed, "And to you, Lew Losoncy, for bundling those bars of Steel at Car Tech, we are here because of your efforts!"

Then I thought about all of the other workers who didn't feel what I felt that day because they didn't have a meaning-giving supervisor like Mr. U.

8   **Use humor to help people accept what they won't change.** Remembering our chapter on Acceptance and Reality, help people to humorously accept that "What is, is!" I ask groups, "If it's 90 degrees and it is snowing outside, should it be snowing? Of course. Why? Because it is! What is, is!"

9   **Build excitement for change by associating change with growth.** There has never been a time when so much change was taking place in so many lives as it is today. And there will be even more tomorrow. In an earlier chapter, we talked about the importance of becoming intrinsically motivated, building a cheerleader inside us, because the outside world is always in transition. We can't count on constancy in the outside world. So we need to build security inside ourselves.

People with practical intelligence, with inner security, realize that not only do they have to adapt quickly to change, but they need to find ways of welcoming and embracing change and finding refreshment and personal growth in change.

Have you experienced the looks on the faces of people who resist change? Arms-folded, heads-down people who haven't developed their practical intelligence turn their frustration into anger and sometimes even paranoia. Can you recall going to a picnic and watching an 80 year-old woman dancing to Britney Spears music outside in the hot pavilion, while some others waved their hands in disgust, saying, "Look at her, dancing to that crazy music?" She welcomed change. And was rewarded for it.

Wouldn't you like to be like her when you are 80? Are you listening to the music of today and trying to understand it? Or do you remind yourself of your own mother and father responding to your music when you were a teen?

What changes do you face today? How can you develop your practical intelligence and find a way to make it refreshing?

Who do you know that needs some of your encouragement to get a new view of things to help them through some tough changing times.

Bob Dylan was right when he said that "the times they are a changing." The times are always a-changing.

10 Give credit rather than taking credit.
President Ronald Reagan had a sign on his desk that read, "Nothing is impossible for the person who doesn't mind if someone else gets the credit."

So true. Make it a practice to be a credit giver, rather than a credit hog. If you have an idea, and someone else suggests it, resist the tendency to say, "I've been thinking of that for a long while." Instead respond, "What a great idea. How do you see us getting that started?"

My friend, Gust Zogas, is a master of giving credit. Gust is the longest lasting President of Pennsylvania Community Colleges. He pulled off an impossible expansion of an institution that was once rejected by taxpayers. It's now a place that has touched every single family in Reading, Pennsylvania. Gust works with people to get things done by involving their ideas, by getting them to buy in and commit, and then by spending most of the time giving the credit to those people. Everyone knows Gust will give you a fair shake. After decades of leadership and the right to have buildings named after him, Gust simply tells you that he didn't do anything. It was the great citizens of Berks County who built this phenomenon called RACC.

Some say "Be like Mike." I say, "Be like Gust!" Give credit and let credit come back to you in the form of inner satisfaction and outer achievement.

11 Use enthusiastic, upbeat words. The words we use are crucial in encouragement. Use words that create a winning, on-the-move, active, find-a-way feeling. Our words can be the propellants that stimulate the minds and hearts

of people up over the hills and obstacles along the way. After reading the following group of words, record your reactions:

closed

stale

dead

stagnant

same

common

lifeless

rut

boring

decayed

routine

ho-hum

Your reactions: _____

_____

_____

_____

_____

_____

Now record your reactions after reading these words:

crisp

on-the-move

uplifting

high

fresh

youthful

birth

bigger

original

new

ascend

virile

debut

prime

Your reactions: _____

_____

_____

_____

_____

_____

There is a huge difference between telling a group "Things look bad" than taking the same situation and saying, "We face an exciting challenge ahead of us. We are about to see our best days."

ENCOURAGE PEOPLE TO THINK ABOUT THESE QUESTIONS OR
There must be 50 ways to find more meaning at work

Personal Meaning

1. **Personal Growth:** How have I grown since I started with the company?

2. **Pride:** What accomplishments do I feel most proud about in doing what I do?

3. **Self-esteem:** How has my work changed my belief in myself through the years?

4. **Creativity:** When did I put my own ideas into my work that was meaningful?

5. **Security:** What security have I earned through my years on the job?

6. **Love:** What do I love most about my job?

7. **Courage:** What was my most courageous moment on the job?

8. **Challenge:** What is my biggest challenge today? How can I turn it into a positive?

9. **Vision:** What personal quality will I develop this year?

10. **Curiosity:** How can I use my curiosity to grow even further on the job?

Task Meaning

11. **Skill Refinement:** What skills have I developed since being here at the company?

12. **Task Mastery Over Specific Tasks:** What have I learned to master, to do really well? Maybe I'm one of the best there is.

13. **Task Progress:** What area of my work am I progressing at the most, perhaps because I've been opened to learn?

14. **Correction:** What was a significant moment when I learned a better way to do what I was doing and I improved myself?

15. **Problem Solving:** What problem did the company have that I helped to solve?

16. **Future Improvement:** What task do I need to work on to make my future even better?

Career/ Professional Meaning

17. **Professional Growth:** How have I grown, not personally, but professionally since being with the company?

18. **Previous Job Mastery:** What previous jobs have I had to learn and master?

19. **Recognition:** What recognition have I received from my work?

20. **Advancement:** What advancements have I made since I started with the company?

21. **Future Career Advancements:** What am I willing to work toward to make my future even better than today?

Social Meaning

22. **Rewarding Relationships:** What rewarding relationships have I found here at the company?

23. **Attention:** Who notices me? Who offers support when I need it?

24. **Belonging:** To which group do I feel I belong?

25. **Contributing:** Who have I helped to become better?

26. **Encouraging:** Who do I believe in or have supported?

Team Meaning

27. **Mutual Respect:** Who on the team do I respect. Who in return respects me?

28. **Mutual Progress:** Who in the company is growing along with me?

29. **Synergy of Ideas:** Who on the team do I brainstorm new ideas with and things just flow?

30. **Team Theming:** What makes our team special? How are we unique?

31. **Winning Team:** What have we accomplished together?

32. **Open Communications:** Who can I tell both good and bad news about our work? Who can I be extremely honest with when recommending better ways to improve our work?

33. **Contributing at a Team Level:** How have I made our team better?

Organizational Meaning

34. **Fulfilling Vision:** How am I helping fulfill the company's vision?

35. **Living Cultural Values:** What is an example of when I truly lived the company's values?

36. **Feeling Empowered:** In what areas do I feel the company trusts me to trust myself?

37. **Being the Difference:** How have I made a difference for the company?

38. **Future Contribution:** What can I do that I know the company needs to make it a better place?

Customer Meaning

39. **Customer Sensitivity:** When I walk a mile in customers' shoes, what am I most aware of?

40. **Striving for Perfection in Services:** What are some examples of times when I fought for the customer?

41. **Customer Humanizing:** When did I consciously treat a customer as a unique, special, distinct, important human being rather than just a number? What were the results?

Community Meaning

42. **Community Development:** How have I, through my work, made my community a better place?

43. **Professional Community:** In what ways have I advanced my profession in my community's eyes?

World Meaning

44. **Building a Better World:** What is the single thing that sticks out in my mind as to how I am building a better world?

45. **Touching Lives:** How many lives have I touched, directly or indirectly, through my work since being with the company?

Inspirational Meaning

46. **Self-Actualizing at Work:** Where in my work am I moving toward becoming the person I am capable of becoming?

47. **Flow:** When am I the most myself in my job, or when am I truly in a state of flow, lost in my work?

48. **Spirit:** What gives me the most satisfaction about my work? What brings my spirit to life?

49. **Passion:** What do I believe in, more than anything else, about my work?

50. **God at Work:** How am I inspiring a better universe and connecting to God, or my equivalent to the ultimate, through my work?

Encouraging is better than blaming because encouragement communicates belief and hope. Consider those people closest to you and develop a plan to lift them up and bring them in. When you encourage someone, you change their world—and yours.

Now, let's explore ways of developing your practical intelligence by keeping your own self going and growing, buoyed up by an optimistic approach to life.

7

OPTIMISM

*Lifts Us More
Than Blaming Our
Challenges*

Every human achievement started in the mind and heart of a spirited individual who believed that the dream could be realized. Humanity has progressed from living in caves, to climbing snow-packed mountains that soar almost five miles into the heavens, to living in vehicles that travel around the earth in a hour, to placing a flag on the moon. For centuries, optimists have cured diseases that plague the human body, but not those that destroy the human spirit.

All of these achievements, and more, have been accomplished because of a few believers who had an eye on the heavens and a desire for improvement. They had a huge advantage. They were optimists.

Every success story has one thing in common—people who operate out of deep conviction that every problem has a solution. In fact, every problem has many solutions—as many solution as there are optimistic people who are willing to lift their chins up and seek success. Bertrand Russell enlightened us with his conclusion that, "In the vast realm of the alive, creative, human mind there were no limitations."

OPTIMISTS LOOK AT WHAT THEY CAN DO AND DO IT. PESSIMISTS LOOK AT WHAT THEY CAN'T OR WON'T DO AND GET FRUSTRATED

After graduating from college, I was a fifth grade teacher for a year. All enthused to teach, it wasn't long before my fires were dampened toward teaching. At lunch time, in the faculty room, I was listening to some teachers talking about the futility of education.

"These kids nowadays don't care. They're not like we were in our day. They just don't want to learn."

Another added, "And parents don't give you as a teacher any support today either. In my day if I went home and told my parents the teacher yelled at me, I'd get a good spanking."

It went on and on. "The school district doesn't respect its teachers today, either. The school board doesn't want to pay us what we are worth. They treat us like trash. Teaching is not like it used to be."

Listening to a litany of blames, I allowed myself to be sucked into the pain of professional uselessness. I left the faculty room and walked down the hallway thinking about quitting teaching at the end of the year and maybe becoming a weatherman or something. By the way I was walking, it must have looked like I was down and out. I felt a tap on my shoulder. When I looked back, there was one of the happiest teachers in the school.

"What's the matter? It looks like you lost your best friend."

"What's the point of teaching?" I said, echoing the sentiment in the faculty room.

"Kids today don't care, the parents are against you, the school district doesn't support you, and the school board doesn't want to pay us what we are worth."

The wise teacher smiled, took a folded newspaper from under his arm, and pointed it at me as if to instruct. With the school bell ringing in the background, he asked, "Where you just in the faculty room?"

I responded, "Yes, how did you know?"

He answered, "You sound just like them. Kid, you don't have to change these kid's pasts. You don't have to influence their parents. You don't have to be concerned about the school district, the school board, or for that matter the President of the United States. All you have to do is to have a great day with those 25 children who are with you this year. You have a year with 25 little human beings that you can help believe in themselves. That's all. You are making your life too tough."

He smiled and walked down the hallway. I heard him say to his class, "In the next 45 minutes, you are going to learn how airplanes fly and you will remember it for the rest of your life. Are you ready?"

"Yeah!"

This teacher's view of life worked better than the faculty room pessimists. His view changed my life because he helped me to focus on what I can do, not what I can't or won't do.

IMPROVE YOUR VISION

It's all in the way you look at things. If your power system, your zest for life, is turned off, you can easily ignite the engines again by changing your attitude. Become your own optometrist today and make a decision to clear up your vision. Put on an enthusiastic set of eyeglasses in order to view yourself, other people, and the world in a new way.

The philosopher William James proclaimed that the greatest revolution of the century was the discovery that human beings, by changing the inner view of themselves in their minds, could change their outer world. Think of it. By changing the way you look at things, through your new set of eyeglasses toward life, you can actually change your life. The incredible story of William James, surely one of the most popular philosophers of all times, is a perfect example of the power of a person's view of life.

James had severe depression and was even suicidal at times. James, like many people today, pondered the uselessness of his life, often seeing no reason to go on. He was pessimistic, believing that nothing really seemed to matter. James concluded that it was useless to work harder at life if nothing really mattered anyway.

In a letter to a friend, James expressed his hopeless, "what's the use?" view of things. He described his fatalistic outlook on life and his belief that everything was predetermined. The return letter from his friend literally changed the academic world for decades just by changing James' view of his life. In that life-changing letter, his friend urged him to wake up in the morning, set a goal, make a commitment to the goal, and by day's end to see if that worked better than a pessimistic approach that nothing affects your life.

James took his friend's advice. The next day, James started his winning streak on a optimistic note by changing his view of his day. Instead of believing that he was powerless and that nothing mattered, he concluded it was up to him to create his own optimism. This new view gave him the enthusiasm and energy necessary to meet the challenges of the day. With his new life outlook, or inlook, his life changed dramatically. William James then began making monumental contributions to the disciplines of psychology and philosophy. In fact, James went on to help develop one of the major schools of philosophy called pragmatism.

Not coincidentally, pragmatism is the idea that truth is simply the process of finding beliefs that work. His previous hopeless, negative ideas about life didn't work. Remember the pessimistic teachers in the faculty room whose negative ideas about life were causing them misery? Their ideas, no matter how accurate they were or weren't, didn't work to give them meaning and motivation or enthusiasm and energy.

When William James made a commitment each day to approach the day with optimism toward his life and his work, the new belief worked and he became productive. James became his own optometrist, changed his set of eyeglasses toward life, and his life changed.

What does this mean to you? You give yourself a huge advantage when you wake up and make a commitment to proceeding optimistically toward the day.

CULTIVATE A PHILOSOPHY OF LIFE THAT WORKS

The poet Samuel Johnson wrote, "When there is no hope, there can be no endeavor." Hopelessness and pessimism create a fast downhill freefall. Hope and optimism are the fuels to power you past any cloudy weather. When looking up, look beyond the clouds and you will seeing the shining sun.

The sun is always there, but during a rainstorm in life, only the optimists see it.

Optimism is a better predictor of a person's positive motivation than is intelligence. In fact, sometimes intelligence and overanalyzing gets in the way of getting things done. I recall being invited to participate in a noontime debate on a TV program. It was entitled, *"Life in the Late 70's: The Best or Worst Time to Live?"* I was going to debate someone who I believe was one of the most brilliant people I had ever met.

Prior to the 10-minute debate, I had the opportunity to spend a bit of time in the studio waiting room with my debate opponent, an advocate of fatalistic foundations. Even in the waiting room, his face wore a bitter, hopeless expression. To break the ice, I asked my opponent how long he thought he could talk about how horrible life was in the 70s. He responded that he could probably go on forever about how bad things were. He talked about injustices, economic atrocities, political pilfering, natural disasters, educational inefficiencies, and moral decay. The genius of gloom went on to say that he had accumulated enough data to suggest that this was the worst time ever in the history of humankind to live.

At this point, a few minutes away from the actual debate, I glanced at my opponent's reams of discouraging data. Not having a single jotting to support my positive position, I felt a surge of unpreparedness. Because it was obvious that he had more information to present than I did, I offered my friend the opportunity to take some of my 5 minutes, along with his 5 to present his position. Without hesitation, he agreed to take not only his debate time, but 4 and a half minutes of my time. I would take the last 30 seconds.

A few minutes later, it was time for the debate to begin. The host explained the unusual procedure the debate was to follow and then introduced the purveyor of the pessimistic perspective. The professor's presentation commenced, and in only a few seconds it was obvious about how well versed he was on the topic. It seemed like he had spent a lifetime accumulating data to support the bleak view of life. His data was impeccable, his content was well organized, and his delivery was congruent with the facts. His topic on how life was channeled onto a catastrophic course was so effective, I have to admit that at moments in his monologue I felt sympathetic misery, sometimes angry, despaired, and hopeless. His presentation only missed having background music like "Eve of Destruction" playing.

My time finally arrived. I took part of my 30 seconds commending him for his eye-opening presentation. I then turned to the professor with the question, "Sir, does the view that you choose to give to your life work best? Does it make you happy and productive?

Does your view of life work for you? If it doesn't, sounds like there's no downside risk in developing a new view. To be successful, it is important to realize that our view is more important than the facts. And the significant realization is not how intelligent you are, but rather how you can use your IQ to make things better. Using your intelligence as the professor did, to gather data about how bad things are, is unproductive, busywork that certainly cannot make one happy. All of the negative data about life that can be amassed is sterile in the mind of a positive enthusiast who believes things can get better and quickly moves to make things happen. The professor's ideas were accurate, but they didn't work. Create an outlook on life that works and make a difference by proceeding optimistically. And when we proceed optimistically, we are going forward lifted up with the conviction that our problems have solutions.

The history of humankind reminds us that there have always been problems to challenge the human mind and heart and that there were always people, most people in fact, who responded to these problems by griping, whining, blaming, complaining, and giving up. And then there were others who saw the same problems, fired up their optimistic determination and looked for solutions. It is a simple fact that humankind has progressed because of these rare, but treasured optimists, who, despite the odds, rejected the useless course of worrying or wallowing in the dreaded course of pessimism. That's why you don't have any streets in your hometown named after pessimists and you probably have never been to a testimonial dinner for a nit picker.

PUT YOUR POSITIVE VIEW INTO ACTION

An optimist, even under the most difficult outside challenges, knows that the only challenge in life within one's own self. The challenge is to go on and on. Such a positive doer was Terry Fox. The young, handsome Canadian, at the height of his athletic career, was told that he had cancer in his right leg. The disease was rapidly spreading toward other parts of his body, forcing the need to amputate his leg. The sudden news shattered Terry's original lifetime dreams.

Terry Fox had to make a choice: blame the world or make something happen? Which course do you think is more likely to work?

Instead of running away, the optimistic young man began the "Marathon of Hope" to help raise funds for cancer research. He took on the challenge of literally running, with the assistance of an artificial leg, from Eastern to Western Canada, a distance of over 3,000 miles. Unfortunately Terry didn't succeed in reaching Vancouver because the cancer in his leg had spread to his lungs and eventually to the rest of his body. After running halfway across the continent, he was hospitalized and died shortly afterward.

But Terry Fox did succeed in other ways. He not only raised millions of dollars for cancer research, but he inspired all Canadians and others throughout the world with the truth that we can overcome our challenges, first by believing and second by showing up and doing. He made us all realize that we all count. Terry brought people together to work toward common goals, and he brought goodness out in all of us.

"Somewhere the hurting must stop," Terry hoped. Cancer will be beaten someday because of people like Terry.

You might say that the optimist who takes action always has a leg to stand on.

OPTIMISTS WHO TAKE ACTION LIVE ON

One optimist who got things done was Irwin Westheimer. The year was 1909. While at work one morning, the 23-year-old man glanced through his office window and observed a young boy searching through a garbage can for food. Irwin Westheimer was touched, but more practically, he was determined to take action. A pessimist might decry the social injustices or even envision the doom of humankind over an additional glass of wine. Not Irwin. He went out to bring the boy into his office. Irwin fed the boy, went to the boy's home to meet his mother, and eventually found employment for her. But the young optimist didn't stop there. Irwin went to the members of his club and encouraged each of them to do the same with other impoverished youth in the community.

At age 101 Irwin Westheimer died. Or did he? No, because he continues to live in the hearts of a half million boys who are still being touched by his optimistically based actions. These fatherless boys feel a sense of importance each time they play catch with a "Big Brother." Irwin Westheimer was the founder of the Big Brothers of America. Surely thousands of people see or read about children eating out of garbage cans. But Irwin was a doer, who saw the problem and moved toward a solution.

OPTIMISTS GO ON
EVEN AGAINST ALL ODDS

Another optimist who made a huge difference was Marva Collins. She is a Chicago school leader, an optimistic doer. Frustrated by the public schools, she formed her own school, the Westside Preparatory School. Soon after her school opened, she had sixth graders who were reading at college level. She threw away the "See Spot Run" books and introduced elementary school children to Shakespeare, Plato, Aristotle, Emerson, and other classic writers. A powerful achievement, wouldn't you say?

Yes, but the achievement is even more powerful than that. You see, Westside accepts only those students who are either expelled or are failing miserably in the public schools. The student body at Westside is composed of children who are labeled either "mentally retarded," "incorrigible," or having some form of learning disability.

Initially, Marva Collins used her home on Chicago's tough westside as the classroom for 18 pupils. In 5 years time, she had 200 pupils aged 4–14, and 7 teachers housed in a school building with 6 classrooms. Westside currently has a waiting list of several thousand.

All of this was because of one person. Marva Collins saw a problem, took action, and made a difference against all odds. Again, if she hadn't acted on hope, there would not have been any.

The world is a better place because of Terry Fox, Irwin Westheimer, and Marva Collins—and hopefully because of you.

DEVELOPING YOUR OPTIMISTIC EXPLANATORY STYLE

A form of practical intelligence is the ability to find the most workable view to handle setbacks. In his book, **Learned Optimism**, Philadelphia psychologist Dr. Martin Seligman outlined a breakthrough concept on optimism. Seligman observed that optimists and pessimists explain setbacks to themselves in different ways. He called the way we explain a setback our "explanatory style." Seligman's ideas are powerful and can change your life in one reading.

There are three major differences in how optimists and pessimists explain a setback to themselves. Pessimists tend to take the viewpoint that setbacks are personal, permanent, and pervasive. That is, when something happens to a pessimist, such as a rejection or not getting a job, the pessimist concludes: (1) "I'm no good" (personal), (2) "I'll never be any good" (permanent), and (3) "I'll never be able to do anything right" (pervasive).

Imagine how you would feel if every time you experienced a setback, you took these three viewpoints from your experience. Would you ever be motivated to try anything again? There's not much practical intelligence in a negative explanatory style because it doesn't work to advance anyone.

The positive person, or the optimist, tends to choose a different explanatory style to respond to the very same setback. The optimist, after reflection, takes these three vantage points: (1) "The situation wasn't right" (situation related, rather than personal, (2) "I'll get the next job" (temporary, rather than permanent), (3) "It won't affect any other area of my life" (situation related rather than pervasive).

Imagine the lifting advantage that having an optimistic explanatory style can offer. By viewing a setback as an optimist does, we urge ourselves to go forward, rather than to catastrophize and give up. Please read Seligman's many books and you will develop your practical intelligence.

Your beliefs shape your destiny. The optimist who holds go-forward beliefs goes forward. There is no downside risk to being an optimist!

USE THE BEST AS MODELS FOR YOUR LIFE

Abraham Maslow transformed the thoughts of the community of psychologists when he outright challenged the ideas of Sigmund Freud about the possibilities of people. Freud, who worked with very seriously disturbed humans a hundred years ago, was pessimistic about the human's ability to rise above their limited biology. Maslow decided to find other models to draw from and studied the healthiest, most fulfilled humans. He called then, "self-actualized." Like a seed becoming a giant oak, when in an actualizing state, humans are able to fully express themselves. They use more of their potential. You could say that they have really developed their practical intelligence because their use of their fuller potential works a lot better than operating out of our lower view of self.

In *The Farther Reaches of Human Nature,* Maslow wrote:

> *"If you want to answer the question as to how tall the human species can grow, then obviously it is wise to pick out the ones who are already the tallest and study them. If we want to know how fast a human can run, then it is of no use to average out the speed of a sample of the population; it is far better to collect Olympic gold medal winners and see how well they can do. If we want to know the possibilities for spiritual growth, value growth or moral development in human beings, then I maintain that we can learn the most by studying our most moral, ethical and saintly people."*

> *"I think that it is fair to say that human history is a record of the ways in which human nature has been sold short. The highest possibilities of human nature have practically always been underrated. Even when good specimens, the saints, the sages, the great leaders of history, have been available for study, the temptation has been too often to consider them not human, but supernaturally endowed."*

Build your practical intelligence. Identify with the best, not the average. Surround yourself with people who have the qualities you want to develop.

OPTIMISTS MOVE TO POSITIVE CLIMATES

The best way to learn French is to live in France for a few years and to associate with French-speaking people. Associate with people who have the qualities you want to acquire. Never get advice from someone who hasn't achieved what you'd like to achieve. Don't go to a down-and-out person who is constantly blaming the world and ask them for advice. Don't ask someone who hates their work, "What's your secret?" They don't know.

If you want to be a millionaire, and you wonder if it is possible, don't ask someone who is bankrupt. They will tell you, "no!" But what happens if you ask the same question to a millionaire. The response will be, "Yes, of course!"

Be careful where you get your advice. Move yourself in circles that have positive climates.

APPOINT A HONORARY BOARD
OF POSITIVE ADVISORS FOR YOURSELF

Remember that you are the CEO of your life. You are also the Director of Environmental Engineering. Hire uplifting people who have developed their practical intelligence—people whose philosophy of life works. Here is a list of people I would turn to, imagining what they would do if faced with the situations that I am facing. They can be living or not and in many instances, I have not even met them. But I sure get a lift when I mentally bring them into my office and ask each one individually, what is your advice for me?

Dr. Jonas Salk, found the cure for polio

Arnie and Sydell Miller, founders of Matrix Essentials

Michael Jordan, athlete

Al Neuharth, founder *USA Today* Newspaper

Dr. Richard Cahn, friend and professor at Kutztown University

John Kennedy, former President

Lance Armstrong, motivator

Elizabeth Marshall, aunt, stand-up comedienne

Make up your own list of Optimistic Board Members:

BOARD OF POSITIVE ADVISORS

1. _____

2. _____

3. _____

4. _____

5. _____

IF YOU CAN'T DO EVERYTHING, DO SOMETHING

What would you like to achieve during your lifetime? What challenges in the world would you like to make a commitment to overcome? How would you like to make the world a better place?

What is your plan? What first step would you like to take? When will you take it?

FIND A WAY TO YOUR DREAMS—JUST BECAUSE SOMETHING IS IMPOSSIBLE DOESN'T MEAN IT CAN'T BE DONE

At times, the word "impossible" has a way of intimidating even the best in us. I guess it's because "impossible" sounds absolute, unbending, and immovable. In actuality, impossible is a relative term.

The "impossible" is relative to time and technology. A hundred years ago, if someone had said a spacecraft would fly a quarter million miles to the moon and a person would walk out and place a flag into the moon's surface, everyone would have thought that was impossible.

Yes, the impossible is relative to time and technology. But mainly, the impossible is relative to an individual's creative determination and find-a-way spirit! The possible is not defined by what lies outside us, but by what lies inside us. The major choice people make in life is to whether or not they want to spend their life energies finding things to blame for why they can't get ahead or using their time to challenge themselves onward to greater achievements.

When you are dreaming of the possible inside yourself, confront the part of you that is looking to blame, look up to the star lit sky, and in the center you'll see the illuminated moon. Then remind yourself that there is a flag on the moon. The challenge ahead of you may be impossible. But just because its impossible, doesn't mean it can't be done. It means the world needs you to do it.

Develop your practical intelligence by choosing a view of life that will work to keep you going. Optimism is a big part of that commitment.

You have a choice: you can blame or you can build!

Which choice tomorrow will you wish you had made today.

REFERENCES

Csikszentmihalyi, Mihaly. *Flow: The Psychology of Optimal Experience*. New York: Harper & Row, 1990.

Dinkmeyer, Don & Losoncy, Lewis. *Skills of Encouragement: How to Bring Out The Best in Yourself and Others*. Boca Raton, Florida: St. Lucie Press, 1996.

Ellis, Albert and Robert Harper. **A New Guide to Rational Living.** Hollywood, California: Wilshire Books, 1975.

Kohn, Alfie. *The Brighter Side of Human Nature*. New York: Basic Books, 1990.

Losoncy, Lewis. *The Motivating Team Leader.* Boca Raton, Florida: St. Lucie Press, 1995.

Losoncy, Lewis. *Turning People On: How to Be an Encouraging Person.* Sanford, Florida. InSync Communications, 2000.

Losoncy, Lewis and Diane Losoncy. *What is, is: How to Accept What You Can't Change & Change What You Can*. Boca Raton, Florida: St. Lucie Press, 1997.

Maslow, Abraham. *The Farther Reaches of Human Nature.* New York: Viking Press, 1971.

Rogers, Carl. *On Becoming a Person.* Boston: Houghton-Mifflin, 1961.

The Diogenes Consortium

**If you found this book thought provoking...
If you are interested in having this author...
or other of our consulting authors
design a workshop or seminar for your
company, organization, school, or team...**

Let the experienced and knowledgeable group of experts at *The Diogenes Consortium* go to work for you. With literally hundreds of years of combined experience in:

*Human Resources • Employee Retention
• Career Planning and Decision Making • Surviving Downsizing
• Pro-Active Leadership • Teams • Encouragement • Empowerment
• Motivation & Energizing Employees • Customer Service
• Misemployment • Coaching • Hiring Strategies and Practices
• Ethics • Spirituality in the Workplace • Pain Management
• Caregiving • End-of-Life Issues • Christian Financial Planning
• Parenting*

*Presentations to start-ups and Fortune 100 companies, tax-exempt
organizations and schools (public & private, elementary through
university) religious groups and organizations*

Visit our website for more information and a list of our great speakers:
http://www.focusonethics.com/thediogenesconsortium.html

Call toll free at: (866) 602-1476

Or write to us at:
2445 River Tree Circle
Sanford, FL 32771